"Robin Cox has brought together a lifetime of Christian devotion and understanding of young people and their challenges in this work. He shares experiences, anecdotes, examples, and quotations from a variety of sources which enrich and illustrate the seven qualities of the title. The wealth and variety of information is clearly and simply presented to assist and empower teachers everywhere, both young and experienced. The work is deeply spiritual; the counsel contemporary, practical, and universal."

—E. L. (Libby) Huggett
Former Deputy Principal, St Mary's School for Girls, Waverley, Johannesburg

"Sometimes if a book isn't available you have to write it yourself. Robin Cox has done just that with this one. He has condensed the wisdom acquired from decades of learning, teaching, and mentoring into what could be described as an essential guide for Christian teachers. Each short chapter brims with the promise of treasure to be discovered if we will only take it to heart and apply it to our practice."

—Graham Coyle
Chairman, European Educators' Christian Association, England

"In an increasingly complex educational landscape, this book provides a wonderful foundation upon which all educators can refer to for guidance, inspiration, and some well-grounded practical strategies. Robin has acquired a significant body of knowledge over a long and distinguished career, and we are now privileged to be able to share in this, so that we too may play a role in the education of both teachers and students. Thank you, Robin!"

—Damien Barry
Regional Principal, OneSchool Global, Tasmania and Queensland

"In these times of climate change, global turmoil, and mental health issues, this book is a pivotal investigation into the necessity for critical support for the youth of the world. Robin Cox's 'whanau'—the world he has known so well as scholar, sports' coach, academic, and mentor—is presented as a challenge to all teachers who in their servant-leadership role, may, in walking in his shoes, ultimately stand enriched through studying the authenticity of his ideals."

—**Hugh Huggett**
Head of English and Staff Executive, St Stithians College, South Africa

"Every teacher at some stage in their career will question whether what they are doing is really worth it or making a difference. This book certainly helps answer that question by reminding us that teaching is a divine calling and part of God's mission. Full of inspiration, real life stories, and biblical encouragement, it certainly meets the author's goal of being a user-friendly book for Christian educators that refocuses its readers on the greatest teacher of all time, Jesus."

—**Nigel Winder**
Children and Families Team Leader, Scripture Union New Zealand

"*7 Key Qualities of Effective Teachers* by Robin Cox is an overdue, rich, and inspiring resource for educators—and in fact for leaders in any organization. The seven qualities and the seventy-two practical strategies give shape to the core concept—how to be an authentic person, an effective leader, a transformative influencer, and how to do that in a way that is based on the way Jesus modeled. I highly recommend this rich resource as a daily text to delve into, to reflect on, to apply as we lead those entrusted to our care, whether they be young people or adults to whom we provide leadership."

—**Rudi Pakendorf**
Educator and business consultant, Wisconsin

7 Key Qualities of Effective Teachers

7 Key Qualities of Effective Teachers

Encouragement for Christian Educators

Robin Cox

foreword by Paul Browning

RESOURCE *Publications* · Eugene, Oregon

7 KEY QUALITIES OF EFFECTIVE TEACHERS
Encouragement for Christian Educators

Resource Publications
An Imprint of Wipf and Stock Publishers
199 W. 8th Ave., Suite 3
Eugene, OR 97401

www.wipfandstock.com

PAPERBACK ISBN: 978-1-7252-5333-9
HARDCOVER ISBN: 978-1-7252-5334-6
EBOOK ISBN: 978-1-7252-5335-3

Manufactured in the U.S.A.   DECEMBER 23, 2019

ALSO BY ROBIN COX

The Mentoring Spirit of the Teacher—Inspiration, support and guidance for aspiring and practising teacher-mentors

Expanding the Spirit of Mentoring—Simple steps and fun activities for a flourishing peer mentor or peer support program

Nurturing the Spirit of Mentoring—50 fun activities for young people and for peer mentor training

Encouraging the Spirit of Mentoring—50 fun activities for the ongoing training of teacher-mentors, volunteer mentors, student leaders, peer mentors and youth workers

The Spirit of Mentoring—A manual for adult volunteers

Letter 2 a Teen—Becoming the Best I can Be

Making a Difference—The Teacher-Mentor, the Kids and the M.A.D Project

More information available at www.yess.co.nz

He gives strength to the weary
and increases the power of the weak.
Even youths grow tired and weary
and young men stumble and fall;
but those who hope in the Lord
will renew their strength.
They will soar on wings like eagles;
they will run and not grow weary,
they will walk and not be faint.

—ISAIAH 40:29–31

To Jane, Trish, and Tim,
Thank you for your support, encouragement,
and belief in my life journey.
To all my *amazing* teachers and mentors:
Thank you for believing in me, shaping, molding, inspiring,
and motivating me over many years.

Contents

Foreword

Teaching is a tough job. It can be incredibly rewarding, but also incredibly demanding and, occasionally, demoralizing.

In the last decade, schools and teachers have become more accountable and been placed in the spotlight, blamed for "failing" our young people. At the same time, there has been a dramatic increase in mental illness, particularly anxiety disorder, among youth. If the job of a teacher wasn't complex and demanding enough, to be a Christian teacher in an increasingly secular society has become even more challenging, particularly if you don't work in a faith-based school. This is why this book is so important.

I fear that society has lost sight of what teaching and good schools are all about. A teacher today could easily fall into the trap of believing that their worth is measured by the standardized test scores of their students, rather than the difference they have made to another person's life. I have never had a young person come back to me after they left school and thank me for teaching them to read, but they have thanked me for being there for them or for igniting a passion.

How do I know this? Because, like Robin Cox, I am an educator who loves Jesus. While I am currently the head of one of Australia's internationally recognized independent schools, and before that, the founding head of another large independent school, I am, at my core, a teacher.

I'm not one of those people who always knew they would become a teacher. You might say I was "called" to become a teacher. I think of it more as being led.

You never really know what you want to do with your life when you are at school—such a hard decision to make when you are still so young. My best subjects were mathematics, engineering science, and technical drawing. The obvious option was to become an engineer. I liked the sound of being an aeronautical engineer. I even toyed with the idea of becoming an architect.

At the conclusion of my school journey, I still didn't know what I wanted to do with my life and neither did my two best mates. So we all took the year off study to work. I was a laborer for a surveying company. The experience gave me time to reflect on who I wanted to be and where I wanted to make an impact.

That was the same year that someone at church asked me to teach Sunday School. I reluctantly took on the role but quickly realized that I loved working with young people! The experience of working at a surveying company also showed me what I didn't want to do.

I remember walking into the lounge room of my family home to announce to my parents what I had decided. My mother interjected, "You're going to tell us you're going into the ministry."

"Well yes, and no. I'm going to become a teacher." In my mind, I was going into ministry. God had been working in my life and gently guiding me. Teaching Sunday School showed me that he had bestowed on me certain gifts and talents (which still needed plenty of honing and refinement) that he wanted me to use. I would never find purpose and fulfilment, if I buried these gifts in the ground.

Teaching is a ministry. I am continually astounded by just how many teachers are Christians—people who have committed their lives to Christ, been bestowed particular gifts and are ministering in what you could argue is the most important work you can be called to do: guiding, developing, and transforming the minds and character of the next generation. More Christians than you can imagine are working in secular schools.

My first year of teaching was incredibly challenging. I had twenty-eight five-year-old children. By 11 a.m. of the first day I had exhausted all my lesson plans and ideas. That evening I had never felt so tired. For the first year, I survived on nine cups of coffee a day. That wasn't sustainable. I worked in a non-Christian environment but, remarkably, God had placed a wonderful Christian woman in the classroom with me as my teacher aide. She became my mentor and source of encouragement. Together we started a staff prayer group, which, by the end, had grown to ten in number.

That was thirty years ago. Over those years I have given some great lessons and delivered some terrible ones. My spirit has soared when I have seen a young person "get it" for the first time or leave me a beautiful note at the end of the year to thank me. Conversely, I have had some dark years as I struggled with an incredibly challenging class, or group of parents whose demands I never seemed able to satisfy. There were times I felt like giving up. If this sounds like you, then you must read on.

If I were asked if there is a particular teacher I remember from my school days, I would answer, "Peter Janda." Mr. Janda was my science teacher, but I don't remember him for our science lessons, or for the grades I achieved under his tutelage. I remember him for the conversations and debates we all had about life.

Mr. Janda wasn't a Christian. He was an atheist. His understanding of science and the world was through the lens of atheism and he loved to try and dispel the truth of God. But something remarkable happened to Mr. Janda when I was in eighth grade. He became a Christian and, overnight, our debates on life changed.

Mr. Janda's life-changing experience changed the way he saw teaching. For him it became a true ministry opportunity. I can still clearly see him standing in the front of the class leading a passionate debate about the creation of our world and then pulling me aside at the end of the lesson to ask how I was. His impact on me continues to this day. I never had the opportunity to tell Mr. Janda that, because later that year God took him home.

When we give our lives to Christ, our work becomes our ministry. We are called by God, set apart by him to do good works. We are his. Our fulfillment in life is found when we use the gifts God has given to us to obey his commands: to love him with all our heart, soul and mind, and to love our neighbor as we love ourselves. We glorify God when we seek to reflect his love into the lives of everyone we come across.

But what does a teaching ministry look like and how can you sustain yourself for that work? This is an even more challenging question if you work in a secular school, particularly one that is openly hostile to matters of faith. Robin answers these questions in *7 Key Qualities of Effective Teachers*. Robin's passion for young people and skill as a mentor is obviously divinely bestowed. I had the privilege of working with Robin, a profoundly gifted, wise, and experienced educator, and can attest to his skill. In the following pages, Robin tells his deeply personal and powerful story of becoming a teacher. He was so grateful to his teachers that he committed his life to mentoring others.

As I worked with Robin, I witnessed him not only mentor young people, but also walk alongside teachers who were struggling with their personal or professional life. Some had lost sight of why they chose to become a teacher. Robin's deep empathy, gentle encouragement, extensive experience, and wise counsel lifted them out of that dark place and inspired, motivated, and re-energized their passion for teaching.

If you are lucky enough to be one of the thousands of people mentored by Robin, you will know just how generous he is. *7 Key Qualities of Effective Teachers* is a way for Robin to mentor many more—to mentor you.

Pulling together approximately forty-five years of reading, reflection, and experience as an educator across four countries, Robin shares seven qualities of an effective Christian teacher to encourage and grow your ministry no matter where God has placed you. He encourages you to: get right with God; look to Jesus, the great teacher; live a balanced, healthy life; see Jesus in others; and empower your students to live fulfilling, purposeful lives.

Within each of the seven qualities there are practical strategies you can immediately implement, challenging questions for you to reflect on, scripture to encourage your continued walk with God, and stories of inspirational people who have gone before us. You can use the book as an encouragement, a devotional, or even as a professional growth plan. I know that this book will be a great encouragement as you seek God with all your heart, mind and spirit. It is a reminder of what an extraordinary profession teaching is, how gifted you are by God, and how amazing you are to simply turn up each day ready to shape the young people entrusted to your care. You *are* God's amazing blessing to others.

Dr. Paul Browning
Headmaster, St Paul's School, Brisbane, Australia

The Vision

TEACHERS WORK IN CHALLENGING, constantly changing environments where they often feel overwhelmed and unappreciated by those they serve. Teachers are valuable and their individual and collective contributions to the lives of students, families, and colleagues are significant.

During these formative times of a student's life, the matrices for healthy relationships are shaped—based on realistic self-awareness and empathetic, affirming, faith-filled behavior patterns. These impact marriages, parenting, and whole-life patterns. When parents themselves are broken, a Christian educator is more important than ever.

Christian educators have the authority to positively impact the lives of students and school communities through their transformative attitudes. In these change-agent roles, some probable outcomes—in addition to those mentioned above and which will be dependent on the culture of the particular school environment—may include:

- A safe and caring community, evident by supportive relationships between school personnel, students, their families and extended families or *whanau*[1]

- Inspired and intrinsically motivated students

- Students—and staff colleagues, even families of students—enter into a meaningful relationship with Jesus

1. Whanau: A New Zealand Maori word. An extended family or community of related families who live together in the same area. For more information: https://teara.govt.nz/en/whanau-maori-and-family/page-1.

- Students use their innovative, entrepreneurial, and creative gifts without fear of failure

- Ongoing affirmations of teachers by one another and by school management teams

- A consistent focus, understanding, and support of the health and wellbeing of teachers, which includes manageable stress levels

- Fewer discipline challenges, a reduction in truancy, substance abuse, antisocial behavior, youth suicide, and other youth related mental health issues

- The development of effective communication and relationship-building skills within the school community. For example, more encouragement, empathy, positive peer support, and no judgmental put-downs or bullying

- Families, teachers and students work together to support one another and make a positive difference in their communities

- Students *feel* the unconditional love and care they crave, *feel* that their opinions are valued and listened to, and, as they journey through the confusing years of adolescence, *feel* that their lives have greater meaning and purpose

We are mindful that every teacher is in a different personal space.

We are encouraged to stand tall and Christlike in the grace that embraces our brokenness, conscious of the fact that we *never* walk alone when the Christian faith, globally, is being battered from all sides. The resurrected Jesus, through the power of the Holy Spirit, is with us *every* step of the way: "God has said: 'Never will I leave you; never will I forsake you'" (Heb 13:5).

"How can I do this?" you might be wondering. "Can I do this as a Christian in a secular school?" "How can I show Christian love in a tangible way that does not set me up for abuse?" "How can I do this in a way that will honor God when speaking about faith is not allowed in the classroom?" "How can I do this when we are under so much pressure from management and parents to deliver academic results?"

In moments of frustration and self-doubt, the words of Holocaust survivor and neurologist Viktor Frankel can inspire us: "Everything can be taken from a man or woman but one thing: the last of human freedoms—to choose one's attitude in any given set of circumstances, to choose one's own way."

And, we embrace the life lesson that the apostle Paul shared with the Philippians: "I have learned the secret of being content in any and every situation, whether well fed or hungry, whether living in plenty or in want. I can do all this through him who gives me strength" (Phil 4:12–13).

Who is the student?

A child of God, not a tool of the State.

Who is the teacher?

A guide, not a guard.

What is the faculty?

A community of scholars not a union of mechanics.

Who is the principal?

A master of teaching, not a master of teachers.

What is learning?

A journey, not a destination.

What is discovery?

Questioning the answers, not answering the questions.

What is the process?

Discovering ideas, not covering the content.

What is the goal?

Open minds, not closed issues.

What is the test?

Being and becoming, not remembering and reviving.

What is a school?

Whatever we choose to make it.

—AUTHOR UNKNOWN

When God gives us children he gives us an assignment, and the assignment quite simply is this: to love them uncondi-tionally, value them highly, and prepare them for a role in life in which they will find meaning and purpose.

—SELWYN HUGHES, CHRISTIAN MINISTER

The Call—My Story

Teachers are those who use themselves as bridges, over which they invite their students to cross; then having facilitated their crossing, joyfully collapse, encouraging them to create bridges of their own.
—NIKOS KAZANTZAKIS, WRITER

WHY DID YOU CHOOSE teaching as a career?

Is your career a response to a "calling"? Or did you have an interest in teaching young people and decide to enter the teaching profession, and you happen to be a Christian as well?

For as long as I can remember, I felt that God had called me to teaching.

I decided to become a teacher when I was about eleven. I was recovering from major operations to remove a cancerous growth from my right jawbone. I had undergone radiation treatment for a few months—two-and-a-half times the adult dose. My doctors, who were unsure if they had been able to remove all the cancer, told my parents that I probably had two years to live.

During this time my mother died unexpectedly. She suffered a pulmonary embolism while recovering from a relatively minor operation. Death was quick. My family was thrown into disarray as we came to terms with the enormity of our loss. Unbeknown to me at the time, God would make good on his promise: "For I know the plans I have for you," declares the LORD, "plans to prosper you and not to harm you, plans to give you hope and a future." (Jer 29:11)

My amazing teachers

While undergoing cancer treatment and in the years that followed, some authentic and amazing teachers blessed and encouraged me. They modeled empathy, put up with my nonsense, tolerated my cheekiness, and were far too patient with my academic performance—maybe non-performance would be closer to the truth. They spoke more than enough times to the potential they could see in me and which I struggled to visualize for a long time. They nurtured and guided a shy, disfigured young boy with low self-esteem on an awesome self-discovery and self-empowerment journey for which I shall be eternally grateful.

They identified my passion for sport, the arena in which they would start their work, encouraging me to become the best person I could be once my doctors allowed me to play non-contact sport again.

Peter, my cricket coach, included me in the cricket team. He protected me from possible danger. He used his years of experience as a teacher to help me develop my self-confidence and self-belief as a sportsman. He also drilled into me the importance of teamwork.

John, another teacher, gave me a role as a touch-judge or linesman of the under thirteen rugby union team. I wrote brief match reports, which were placed on the junior school noticeboard. I began to take an interest in writing. My life was gaining meaning and purpose.

Other teachers, coaches and family members fanned my sporting flames, while my academic results remained inconsistent. I eventually graduated from school and achieved state representation in cross-country, cricket, and field hockey, captained school teams, and was appointed school captain (head student) in my final year at school.

My sporting ambitions were curtailed when I was at university because of the increased risk of potentially serious facial damage, a devastating experience at the time. I decided, once over the shock, to become the best teacher and sports coach I could be.

Now that I am retired, I look back on my career with a multitude of wonderful memories—teaching in four countries, coaching and managing sports teams to under-nineteen at international levels, and becoming a school principal at a Christian school and a secular school. I had opportunities to develop peer mentor and peer support programs in three countries and establish youth mentoring programs in New Zealand and Australia.

A key lesson I learned from my school days was that the teachers who positively influenced my life connected with me in the first instance. Some became lifelong friends. They did their best to walk in my shoes for a while as they explored ways to support, encourage, and motivate me. Small wonder, therefore, that my desire to become a teacher never wavered.

Traveling with and without God — years of confusion

Where was God during this journey?

I was educated at an Anglican (Episcopalian) school during the days of apartheid in South Africa and witnessed first-hand the evils of that heresy. The injustices deeply affected me, and the Christian teaching I received at school about "loving my neighbor" (Mark 12:31) had a profound effect on me.

I was confirmed in the school chapel when I was fourteen and took my confirmation seriously. John Stott's book *Basic Christianity*, which we studied in our confirmation class, guided my understanding of the Christian faith to a deeper level.

In the years that followed, my faith walk was inconsistent. Negative peer pressure and the secular world impacted my life choices. My Christian roots, however, were firmly in place. On many occasions I humbled myself before God. He forgave me. "Then Peter came to Jesus and asked, 'Lord, how many times shall I forgive my brother or sister who sins against me? Up to seven times?' Jesus answered: 'I tell you, not seven times, but seventy-seven times'" (Matt 18:21–22).

I was a slow learner.

Discovering a relationship with Jesus

Each time God welcomed me back with open arms, like the father in the parable of the lost son (Luke 15:11–32). The height, length, depth, and width of God's unconditional love and grace remain beyond my comprehension.

One night early in my teaching career, I was struggling to discern my role as a teacher modeling Christian beliefs and values to impressionable adolescents. I fell to my knees and asked Jesus to forgive me, yet again, for the many times I had taken my eyes off him. I made a commitment to do my best to follow him for the rest of my life.

There were no bells, whistles, or wonderful signs.

I felt a peace around me, a feeling I had not experienced before.

I traveled a new road—and there were many bumps and challenging potholes along the way—which taught me the importance of establishing a right relationship with God. I prioritized my daily times of Bible reading, reflection, and prayer. "All Scripture is God-breathed and is useful for teaching, rebuking, correcting and training in righteousness, so that the servant of God may be thoroughly equipped for every good work" (2 Tim 3:16–17).

I learned the importance of being accountable to God and others for the choices I made. I appreciated, through prayer, intercession, and Christian fellowship, Paul's words to the Philippians: "And the peace of God, which transcends all understanding, will guard your hearts and your minds in Christ Jesus" (Phil 4:7).

Most important, though, was the evolving revelation that establishing a right relationship with God is, like teaching, a lifelong ministry. I must be kind, patient, and gentle with myself.

Understanding how to become a transformative teacher

In South Africa during the 1980s and early 1990s, with the prayerful support and encouragement of a number of wonderful Christian opponents of apartheid, I fulfilled what I have always believed was a divinely inspired vision to run non-racial symposia. Approximately 6,000 students and teachers attended these symposia. Participants listened to influential speakers, discussed ways to work together to prepare for a post-apartheid South Africa, debated, dramatized controversial topics, played sport, laughed, and cried together. Lives were enriched—my own included—and changed forever as barriers between races broke down.

These symposia painted a picture of what a future South Africa could look like. I worked with a team of like-minded people, most of whom were students. Symposia participants were encouraged to give practical meaning to the great command of Jesus, "Love your neighbor as yourself" (Mark 12:31), and become positive change-agents—reformers, transformers, innovators, and visionaries—in a country experiencing transition.

The missing link

As I reflected on these challenging times and on my teaching career, I concluded that a vital resource was missing: a user-friendly, short Christian book for teachers like me.

Let me explain.

I often had tough and challenging situations to deal with.

I felt exhausted from the demanding workload.

I had to deal with the guilt of neglecting my family because of my school commitments.

I felt ineffective and helpless as a Christian teacher working within a secular school environment.

The heresy of apartheid frustrated and angered me.

On occasions, I had neither the energy nor desire to deal with an aggressive and demanding parent, student or colleague.

The weight of responsibility on my shoulders, as a school principal, created times of loneliness and dragged me close to burn-out.

As a teacher, I felt the pain and suffering of a student or colleague, and often felt helpless and inadequate.

I was a fallible Christian trying my best to walk with Jesus as his loyal and obedient ambassador. A user-friendly book for Christian educators that contained simple strategies, practical ideas, and encouraging words to motivate and inspire me was needed. This book would give meaning to the final teaching command Jesus gave his disciples: "Therefore, go and make disciples of all nations, baptizing them in the name of the Father and of the Son and of the Holy Spirit, and teaching them to obey everything I have commanded you. And surely I am with you always, to the very end of the age" (Matt 28:19–20).

This book would feed my soul and allow me to open my heart to God's reassuring voice. God would remind me of the height, depth, length, and breadth of his unconditional love for me (Rom 8:38–39). God would also remind me that the spiritual truth that leads to freedom is the truth that I belong not to the world but to him.

Jesus, the greatest teacher who ever lived, would stride ahead of me, be by my side, and walk behind me. If I fixed my eyes on him, I had nothing to fear as he would sustain me, even carry me, when I felt exhausted or overwhelmed.

Finding no such book, I decided to write one. My prayer is that this book will encourage and further equip educators as the transformers so desperately needed in our global community.

How to use this book

You can choose from a variety of approaches:

- Read the book from cover to cover in one relatively short sitting and then refer back to the pages that have grabbed your attention.

- Keep the book by your bed or work space and read a chapter a day or a week.

- Set some time aside and use the book as part of your personal retreat as you spend time with God and seek his direction for your life.

- Share some of the information during your staff devotion.
- Share with teacher trainees and new teachers to encourage them.
- Meet with colleagues and share your thoughts about each chapter.

Practical tips and strategies, reflections, and words of encouragement are shared in these pages. Notes written by students, parents, and colleagues are humbly shared as examples of how God uses broken and imperfect teachers to encourage and transform lives.

Each chapter opens with a prayerful reflection that can be undertaken whenever you choose: before, during, or after you complete the reading of the chapter.

Biblical quotes and references are included in each chapter to encourage your faith journey, which should always be grounded in regular reading of the Bible—God's Word.

The repetition throughout the book is deliberate as we appreciate the importance of taking a holistic teaching attitude into each day. It also enables you to read each chapter as a stand-alone chapter should you choose this approach.

The names of all teachers, students, and parents have been changed to protect their identity, with the exception of my teachers mentioned in this introduction.

7 key qualities of effective teachers

Jesus models both the way we should behave *in* our community without being *of* it, and the meaning of living in the Spirit of Jesus. He offers us reassuring words: "And I will ask the Father, and he will give you another advocate to help you and be with you forever—the Spirit of truth" (John 14:16).

A chapter is devoted to each of the seven key qualities of effective teachers that provide the framework for this book:

1. Relationships

2. Christlikeness

3. Empowerment

4. Empathy

5. Humility

6. Affirmation

7. Teamwork

Each of these qualities is briefly unpacked and considered through the lens of a Christian teacher to reassure us that, no matter how challenging our work environment might be, we *can* positively impact lives, we *are* making a difference, and we are *never* alone.

God's extraordinary servant leaders

Each chapter concludes with examples of how God uses ordinary, imperfect, and fallible individuals to do his extraordinary work. They highlight the importance of the gospel and serve as reminders that we have a responsibility to train disciples. Further information about these "movers and shakers" can be found in libraries and the media.

These stories are shared for two reasons. Firstly, as teachers, we impact the life of every student with whom we interact and invest our time. Any of these students could ultimately become an extraordinary individual—a mover or shaker—doing Christ-centered work with a global impact. Secondly, you might feel a call on your heart to move out of your comfort zone and take your God-given gifts into a new mission field. Maybe one of these stories will inspire you to prayerfully seek God's direction for your life.

A Christlike attitude

A Christlike attitude will positively impact more lives than we might realize. Kate, a young student I encouraged as she battled serious illness, wrote: "Thank you for being such an incredible supporter and guide over the past three years. Your constant help and faith have strengthened me and given me hope an innumerable amount of times. Thank you for always believing in me, praying for me, supporting me, and guiding me to God's love. You've impacted my life in a very positive way and I can't thank you enough for that."

I penned this short daily prayer a few years ago after one of my morning times of Bible reading and prayer:

> Jesus, let me see with your eyes,
> hear with your ears,
> reach out with your hands,
> walk your talk with your feet,
> connect with your heart
> and love with your love.

Let us walk together in the footsteps of Jesus with enthusiasm and commitment, encouraged by these words and, in our brokenness, with humility, take ownership of this truth: Hey, teacher! You *are* amazing!

MOVERS AND SHAKERS

God calls a variety of people to serve him, such as teachers, writers, army commandos, athletes, people in business or trades, politicians, nurses, and missionaries. We have the responsibility to respond to that call and follow him, no matter the cost. As we respond positively to his call, we sow messages of hope and pour out an abundance of unconditional love in a variety of ways.

Anne Sullivan (1866–1936) was a determined and courageous American teacher who spent almost fifty years working alongside Helen Keller, a journey made famous by the film *The*

Miracle Worker. Anne was almost blind herself, yet persevered through a challenging upbringing. Anne's mother died when she was eight. Her father abandoned her two years later. Through Anne's teaching, selfless commitment, and friendship with Helen, the world received the wonderful gifts of Helen Keller, an exceptionally talented blind and deaf woman. Helen Keller was the first deaf-blind woman to earn a Bachelor of Arts degree. She wrote twelve published books, was a prominent political activist and lecturer, and also helped found the American Civil Liberties Union in 1920.

> It is a rare privilege to watch the birth, growth, and first feeble struggles of a living mind; this privilege is mine.
> (Anne Sullivan)

Clive Staples Lewis (1898–1963) was a British novelist, poet, broadcaster, lecturer (at both Oxford and Cambridge Universities), and the author of more than thirty books, which have been translated into more than thirty languages. Well-known books include *The Chronicles of Narnia, The Screwtape Letters, Mere Christianity, Miracles* and *The Problem of Pain.* C.S. Lewis's Christian faith, which took many years to develop, had a significant impact on his writing and his life in general. Well-known author J.R.R. Tolkien was a close friend, who helped bring C.S. Lewis to Christ. The writings of Scottish author, poet, and Christian minister George MacDonald also had a profound impact on C. S. Lewis.

> We must show our Christian colors if we are to be true to Jesus Christ. (C. S. Lewis)

My vocation is grounded in belonging to Jesus, and in the firm conviction that nothing will separate me from the love of Christ. The work we do is nothing more than a means of transforming our love for Christ into something concrete. I didn't have to find Jesus. Jesus found me and chose me. A strong vocation is based on being possessed by Christ . . .

He is the Life that I want to live.

He is the Light that I want to radiate.

He is the Way to the Father.

He is the Love that I want to love.

He is the Joy that I want to share.

He is the Peace that I want to sow.

Jesus is everything to me.

Without him I can do nothing.

Give! Give the love we have all received to those around you. Give until it hurts, because real love hurts. That is why you must love until it hurts. You must love with your time, your hands, and your hearts.

—MOTHER TERESA OF CALCUTTA

To gain a fresh perspective on your world, try actually looking at life through a child's eye.

—THOMAS KINKADE, PAINTER

CHAPTER 1

Relationships

Our task is to hand back Jesus to the world in all his captivating beauty and brilliance.

—JARROD MCKENNA, PASTOR

REFLECTION

REFLECT ON YOUR DAY with gratitude. Ask God to show you the day through his eyes. Think about the work you did and the people you interacted with. How do you feel you served them to the best of your ability? What did you receive from them? Focus on the detail—the small things: a smile, a gentle touch, an affirming nod, an encouraging word, a helping hand, a celebratory moment when a student experienced an "aha!" moment. Thank God for his presence in the detail and for the deep relationship he has with you. Thank him for the relationships you share with family, friends, students, and colleagues.

PRACTICAL STRATEGIES

Are you right with God?
    Are you right with yourself?
    Are you right with the special people in your life?
    Are you right with those under your care?

As you reflect on these challenging questions, be kind to yourself. Remember, too, that evolving life circumstances and diverse commitments place us in different spaces.

Our intimate relationship with God is the cornerstone of our lives.

Throughout the Bible, God builds meaningful relationships with people, role modeled by Jesus who regarded the world as his classroom. Jesus never asked anyone to do or be anything that he had not first demonstrated in his own life.

Jesus, our perfect role model

Early in his ministry Jesus brought together people with different careers, attitudes, and life experiences. There were fishermen, a tax collector, and Simon the Zealot, who disliked tax collectors (Matt 4:18–22; Mark 1:16–20; Luke 5:1–11; John 1:35–51). He trained them for three years. They observed him, traveled with him, were open to his guidance and teaching, prayed with him, and did their best to obey him. Then he sent them out into the local and wider community equipped with the gospel message, prayer and the power of the Holy Spirit to identify and train disciples (Matt 24:35). Eleven of those twelve disciples changed the world at great personal cost. Today, more than two billion people know the name of Jesus.

How was Jesus able to make such a profound impact on the world?

Jesus modeled the importance of being right with God, right with who we are, and right with the special people in our lives *before* we can be right with those entrusted to our care.

Throughout his active ministry Jesus prioritized the importance of having a time of silence and solitude with God. He conversed with God. He stayed focused on God. He reflected on how he was living God's goals for his life. He renewed his soul in daily contact with God. He continually reminded himself that he *belonged* to God and had a divine ministry to fulfill.

Develop a right relationship with God

How much of your life is a reflection of your Lord and Savior, Jesus? How will others know that you are continually developing a right relationship with God?

Hudson Taylor the nineteenth century pioneering missionary to China selflessly achieved so much yet suffered greatly, largely because of his obedient and close relationship with God. He lost family members, was beaten, robbed and ridiculed, yet he reassuringly stated: "God's work done in God's way will never lack God's supplies."

We develop an intimate relationship with God that allows our souls to be nurtured on a daily basis as we grow spiritually, and are empowered to positively influence others. Hudson Taylor and thousands of others will testify how God equips us with the tools we need as transformative teachers and spiritual leaders, able to encourage others to change their behavior or opinions and to consider God's place in their lives.

A right relationship with God allows us to experience an inner peace. We can choose, as Hudson Taylor did, to set time aside each day to read the Bible, meditate on God's Word, pray, and listen to his voice. We strive to obey him and follow the Bible's teaching for our character development. We strengthen our relationship with Jesus, who reminded his disciples: "I am the way and the truth and the life. No one comes to the father except through me" (John 14:6).

Listen to God's voice

How do you hear God's voice as you develop this right relationship with him and, ultimately, with yourself?

- A particular Bible verse stands out or takes on a special power as God speaks directly to your heart (Ps 116:1).

- A picture develops in your mind during your daily time of Bible reading and prayer, or while listening to praise and worship music (Pss 95, 98, 145, 150).

- Thoughts enter your mind and you experience a deep sense of God's divine presence while you are fasting.

- Sometimes God uses a non-believer to speak an important message into your life, so it is important to walk closely with God every second of every day (Ps 32:8; 2 Tim 3:16).

Develop a right relationship with the special people in our lives

How do you prioritize and nurture your relationships with the special people in your life? What do you regard as the most important qualities of a good friendship?

My wake-up call, relatively early in my career, occurred when I was married with two children under the age of four and in a middle management role. When I returned home after another long day at work, my wife asked me if I was married to her or the school.

From that moment we discussed and developed strategies to ensure that family *always* comes first in our lives. For example, we agreed times during the holidays when I could prepare lessons for a new term; we made time for family outings; we sat around the table, gave thanks to God for his many blessings, and had family meals together during which we shared our respective daily experiences. We did our best to ensure that, even if there was a financial sacrifice, one parent was at home when our children's school finished for the day (Prov 22:6, 1 Cor 13:4–7, Ps 103:17–18).

I have shared this family experience with many colleagues and parents over the years as I continually work to develop a right relationship with the special people in my life.

In senior leadership roles I sat with colleagues experiencing challenging issues with their own children. Once was with a colleague whose teenage daughter had committed suicide and a few occasions were with colleagues experiencing marital issues. In regard to this latter situation, I was quick to point out that I am not a marriage counselor.

Mary shared that her husband was considering leaving her and her young family. We discussed her school and other commitments, and the different ways she and her husband were communicating and supporting one another. I shared a "gold nugget" idea I had remembered from a seminar: "Rekindle the fire of your relationship in the early days." This was an opportunity to pause and reflect about the early months of Mary and her husband's relationship after they had met. We handed everything over to God in prayer. I remained in the background during the next few months, quietly supporting Mary, checking on her wellbeing, and praying for the family. Mary and her husband worked through their issues and celebrated their silver wedding anniversary recently. Most important, though, was the deepening of Mary's faith throughout this experience. Mary learned to be gentle and kind to herself while showing greater empathy towards her husband's personality.

Develop a right relationship with others

What does your evolving spiritual leadership look like to others as you develop a right relationship with God, yourself, and the special people in your life?

Jesus models the life of a good shepherd, a spiritual leader. He portrays the level of intimacy necessary for us to have the credibility to positively influence others. In John 10:1–21 Jesus describes the relationship between the good shepherd and the sheep to encourage us to develop that right relationship with him, and with others: "I am the good shepherd; I know my sheep and my sheep know me—just as the Father knows me and I know the Father" (John 10:14–15).

When we display unconditional love towards people, we build value into their lives as the good shepherd displays to his sheep. We model the three core qualities on which meaningful relationships are developed: respect, empathy, and sincerity, as occurred between Philippa and Gerald.

Philippa was an academically gifted fourteen-year-old studying above her years. However, she was out of her depth socially and emotionally as she interacted with her older peers. Philippa was drifting into risk-taking behavior when she spoke to Gerald, one of her teachers. Two years later, at her graduation, she gave Gerald a small gift and a card, inside which she wrote: "I thank you for all the time you took to listen to me and to be there for me, even when I was the complete opposite of the person you believed I could be. You spoke little but said so much and while everyone told me what to do you asked me what I wanted. I still ask myself that question every day, "Is this what I truly want?" In challenging me to answer that question I found courage, peace, meaning, God and faith. Now I can be the real me."

Teachers lead by example

Authentic teachers observe more positive behavior and increased academic achievement when their optimistic personalities support the social and emotional wellbeing of students.

Our students are young people, not projects. Each is unique with a variety of gifts and talents. We shape, refine and mold these students into people who will, hopefully, embrace their communities and make a positive difference. We devote ourselves to their individual and collective needs as we build meaningful relationships with them. We focus on them and not ourselves (Matt 16:24). We teach by modeling what we teach. We never forget that discipleship is more easily caught than taught.

We also experience less stress and are happier when we prioritize our physical and spiritual health.

Develop a right relationship with students

Are you right with the students with whom you interact? What do these relationships look like on a daily basis?

One of the greatest gifts we give others is our individual selves, and we become Christlike shepherds when we design value into our relationships. Jesus reminds us that good shepherds are willing to lay down their lives for their sheep (John 10:11), such is the nature of the unconditional love they display towards the sheep.

The parables of the wandering sheep (Matt 18:10–14), the lost sheep (Luke 15:3–7), and the lost son (Luke 15:11–32), highlight the significant value a forgiving God places on *every* individual. The parables highlight the importance of being in a right relationship with God, with ourselves, with the special people in our lives, and with others.

God views *every* lost person with compassion. He longs for *every* lost person to return to him. He waits as a loving parent waits for their lost or wayward child to return home. In these parables the lost (sinners) return to a place where they will find rest in God's unconditional love, grace, and peace (Luke 15:10). Their relationship with God is strengthened and becomes more intimate.

We experience the "lost" child in our work. For example, the student whose behavior causes us endless grief and frustration as he or she drifts in different directions for a variety of reasons. How do you welcome these students each day? Australian child psychologist, Andrew Fuller, points out that:

> About 45 percent of any school's population have attachment issues. For these students, trust, wariness, hypervigilance, and insecurity are major barriers to learning. Living the core value of happiness, belonging, and safety for all, acts as an antidote to the barriers to learning experienced by insecure or avoidant students.[1]

Happy students are more capable of lateral and creative thinking, important skills for future careers. These students become

1. Fuller, *Re-inventing schools*, 1.

responsible risk-takers and non-conformists when they develop the self-confidence to learn how to express their uniqueness in a safe environment.

Reflect for a moment: *Will* I be a more effective teacher if I make a genuine effort to know the students I teach?

The power of forgiveness

Do you love yourself as a forgiven and grace-filled Christian?

If we are unable to love ourselves as forgiven and grace-filled Christians, we cannot possibly hope to be effective caregivers to others. We might also struggle in our relationships with those colleagues who irritate and annoy us on occasions.

So, what should we do?

We invite Jesus to be the perfector of our faith. He richly blesses us and coaches us how to forgive, and we experience inner freedom and peace. The resurrected Jesus, through the power of the Holy Spirit, enables us to stand tall in the grace that embraces our brokenness. We love ourselves as forgiven and grace-filled Christians conscious of the fact that we *never* walk alone (Josh 1:5).

Jesus equips us with the skills and authority to authentically teach and build meaningful relationships with others. He also guides us and gives meaning to one of the greatest life challenges he lays before us: "A new command I give you: Love one another. As I have loved you, so you must love one another. By this everyone will know that you are my disciples, if you love one another" (John 13:34).

Genuine Christian teachers believe that God brings specific students, their families, and colleagues into their lives as his timing is *always* perfect.

How will you consistently love and support these people to discover their God-given purpose? How will you help them discover and nurture their gifts to bring them fulfillment and bring joy and glory to God?

I remember sensing that God wanted me to speak to Meg, a student I had neither taught nor spent much time with. My role in our relationship became that of a listener and encourager. Meg chased her goals and dreams during a season when she also worked through some challenging peer and family relationship issues. Meg wrote me this note when she completed her schooling: "Thank you for always believing in me and encouraging me to set higher standards for myself, striving further to reach my ambitions. You have had a profound impact on my life and I am so grateful for all the lessons you have taught me (or guided me to)."

Six key relationship-building strategies

Six key relationship-building strategies to prayerfully consider (1 Thess 2:8, John 1:43, John 11:54, Matt 9:9) include:

1. Model the language and behavior you want students to demonstrate and always use respectful language. Share positive thoughts with your students: "I am proud of the way you have worked today." "You make my job such fun!" "You have made my day!" "I knew you could do it." "I love your creativity."

2. Be genuine. Do not put on an act. Your role is to please God, not impress students, parents or colleagues. Sometimes there will be a cost involved—ridicule, rejection, maybe persecution. Courageously set out to reflect God in all you think, do, and say every day (Isa 42:8), as his obedient disciple.

3. Display compassionate authority. Share messages of hope. Encouragement builds upon a person's assets and strengths (Eph 4:29, 5:1). This was evident in Susan and Deb's relationship.

    Susan struggled with past interpersonal relationships and carried a burden of what "should have" or "could have" been done. Regret weighed her down. She had a few conversations with Deb, one of her teachers, about decision-making, the need to move forward, and how God's grace sets us free from the past. Many months later Susan wrote a note to Deb: "I would just like to take the time to thank you for not only being a tremendous teacher, but also a mentor and comforter for me in my time of need. I was able to confide things in you that I couldn't in anyone else and you aided me in my spiritual growth with Christ. Thank you for all the years you have been by my side, as a teacher, and as a friend."

4. Set firm and realistic boundaries in a compassionate and fair way. Consistently promote caring and respectful relationships among all students and staff colleagues.

5. Make people feel important. Correctly pronounce their names. Always respect cultural values. For example, know when and when not to use eye contact or to praise students in public. Learn to listen carefully to understand the viewpoints of others; smile; be friendly, and talk about what interests them (Appendix 1, Ps 37:3). Have an "open door" policy and be approachable if students want to speak to you out of class time. Move from behind your desk and sit alongside a student if you are meeting him or her face-to-face. Deliberately create a more informal atmosphere as you build meaningful relationships with others.

Fifteen-year-old Emma was concerned about the negative peer pressure she was experiencing on social media. She was underperforming academically and beginning to doubt herself when she hesitantly approached me for assistance. We chatted informally for a while as I sought to put her at ease. Soon, as the trust was developed, she began to share her deeper thoughts. I listened, clarified her concerns, and fixed my full attention on her when we met. We put agreed strategies in place, with a particular focus on how she could build meaningful relationships with her peers. A few months later she wrote, "You have been such an inspiration and help and I really am thankful."

Emma excelled in her final two years at school.

Emma's experience gives credence to Dr Helen Street's belief that:

> Positive relationships build students' resiliency and mental health and enhance their capacity for learning.[2]

2. Street, *Contextual Wellbeing*, 109

6. Never quit on your students. Persevere with ideas and explore possibilities. Be prepared to move out of your comfort zone and listen for God's prompts.

MOVERS AND SHAKERS

God takes ordinary people from a variety of backgrounds and experiences and uses them powerfully to share the gospel, sometimes with global consequences.

William (1829–1912) and Catherine (1829–1890) Booth were the founders of the Salvation Army. Both made Christian commitments during their adolescent years. The adolescent William was influenced by a close friend, William Sansom. These teenagers started Mission Ministry. In later years, William and Catherine's relational work was among the poorest of the poor and those struggling with alcohol addiction. The Salvation Army is regarded as one of the largest global distributors of humanitarian aid.

> There is no improving the future without disturbing the present. (Catherine Booth)

> Faith and works should travel side by side, step answering step, like the legs of men walking. First faith, and then works; and then faith again, and then works again—until they can scarcely distinguish which is the one and which is the other. (William Booth)

George Mueller (1805–1898) was a Christian evangelist and the director of the Ashley Down Orphanage in Bristol, England. The son of a tax collector and an unbeliever, George was a wild teenager jailed for stealing at the age of sixteen. He decided to attend a Bible study in 1825, where he met Jesus and began his life-changing spiritual journey. By the time of his death, George had cared for 10,024 orphans and established 117 schools offering a Christian education to more than 120,000 children. His relational legacy continues today. A significant aspect of George's ministry was that he never approached anyone for donations. He never went into debt, depending totally on God to meet his ministry's needs.

> I live in the spirit of prayer. I pray as I walk, when I lie down, and when I rise. And the answers are always coming. Tens of thousands of times my prayers have been answered. When once I am persuaded a thing is right, I go on praying for it until the end comes. I never give up! (George Mueller)

RADIATING CHRIST

Dear Jesus, help me to spread Your fragrance everywhere I go.

Flood my soul with Your spirit and life.

Penetrate and possess my whole being so utterly,

That my life may only be a radiance of Yours.

Shine through me, and be so in me

That every soul I come in contact with

May feel Your presence in my soul.

Let them look up and see no longer me, but only Jesus!

Stay with me and then I shall begin to shine as You shine,

So to shine as to be a light to others;

The light, O Jesus will be all from You; none of it will be mine;

It will be you, shining on others through me.

Let me thus praise You the way You love best, by shining on those around me.

Let me preach You without preaching, not by words but by my example,

By the catching force of the sympathetic influence of what I do,

The evident fullness of the love my heart bears to you. Amen.

—John Henry Cardinal Newman

CHAPTER 2

Christlikeness

Being a Christian is more than just an instantaneous conversion—it is a daily process whereby you grow to be more and more like Christ.

—BILLY GRAHAM, EVANGELIST

REFLECTION

REFLECT ON YOUR DAY and the different feelings you experienced. When did you feel happy, connected with a person or others, challenged, encouraged, comforted, and at peace? Pause and reflect on one moment when you felt most grateful. Thank God for this experience. When did you feel irritable, overwhelmed, alone, sad, or weary? Bring these moments to God. Hand them over to him. Pray for his healing so you can be his faithful disciple within and outside your workplace.

PRACTICAL STRATEGIES

How deeply is your heart connected to the heart of Jesus?

The apostle Paul, speaking to the elders of the church at Ephesus, stated: "I have declared to both Jews and Greeks alike that they must turn to God in repentance and have faith in our Lord Jesus Christ" (Acts 20:21).

One of the key messages of the gospels is for us to become like Jesus. This is a lifelong journey.

> The story of Jesus [is] a narrative of God's redemptive work in the world which often occurs in quiet and mysterious ways. (George L. Sittser, author)

We are more like Jesus when our hearts are connected to his heart and we live in the Spirit of Jesus—more important than simply knowing Jesus and his words—which he describes in Matthew chapters 5 to 7, the Sermon on the Mount. The theme of these chapters is righteousness, or taking the right actions, as followers of Jesus.

We display the characteristics and Spirit of Jesus as we follow his teaching. We express unconditional love and grace in our relationships with others when we are motivated by *his* love (Matt 25:37, 40; Rom 8:14).

> Love is patient, love is kind. It does not envy, it does not boast, it is not proud. It does not dishonor others, it is not self-seeking, it is not easily angered, it keeps no record of wrongs. Love does not delight in evil but rejoices with the truth. It always protects, always trusts, always hopes, always perseveres (1 Cor 13:4–7).

Meet Jesus in the lives of others

Jesus approaches us in the struggling child, or the disabled, lonely, ridiculed and rejected student, the distraught and frustrated parent, and the overwhelmed colleague. There we meet him. He gives us the wisdom, discernment, and the strength to stand tall, Christlike, in the grace that embraces our brokenness (Luke 21:14–15).

In that place we seek to understand the needs of the people around us. We follow the healing and compassionate example of Jesus, who took the time to focus on people as individuals.

We display warmth, genuine care, and emotional support to others. This is challenging at times. We model the importance of impartiality and honesty. We display a great sense of humor when appropriate. Most especially, we can laugh at ourselves, a defining feature of good mental health.

Shortly before Roger a former teaching colleague died of cancer, he placed a comment on a social media platform: "When I stand before God at the end of my life, I would hope that I would not have a single talent left and could say, 'I used up everything you gave me.'"

Terry one of his former students responded: "You believed in me when no one ever did. Much more than just a teacher or coach. Everyone else saw a delinquent, you saw my talent. God bless you, good man. I wish you all the best. You honestly touched my life. Thank you."

At the bottom of the pit

Let us pause and reflect on how God reached down to our deepest pit or place of suffering and lifted us out with his unconditional love.

God offered me mercy and brought hope during a challenging time in my life. He instilled a sense of purpose. As he did this, he taught me the meaning of grace. I am asked to follow his example in the lives of those under my care.

Questions to ask those we move alongside could include: How can I help and support you? How can I be useful to you? How can I help make this better? How can I add value to this? What is your life story? How can I assist you to make your role easier? How can I build value into what you are suggesting or trying to achieve?

Seven key strategies to place Jesus as Lord of our lives

We are powerful signposts pointing others to God when we invite Jesus to be Lord of our lives.

This, remember, is a lifelong journey, so it is important to be kind, gentle, and patient with ourselves as we reflect on these strategies:

1. Converse with God. Read the Bible daily. Prayerfully reflect and meditate on its teaching. This biblical teaching gradually transforms your wellbeing. You become a "living Christ." "I have been crucified with Christ and I no longer live, but Christ lives in me" (Gal 2:20).

   > The Scriptures give us the instructions and information we need in terms of everything involved in finding our salvation and working it out. (Dr Michael Cassidy, evangelist)

2. God empowers and equips you to live like Christ when you keep your focus on him. Submit to and be filled with the power of the Holy Spirit (John 14:16, 26; 15:26). You become a healing presence in the lives of others (Luke 6:19).

3. Develop a powerful Christlike vision to make positive memories for other people. Reflect on questions like: Where am I going? How am I planning to get there? Why am I doing it? Who can help me get there? How do I model Jesus to my community? Who am I in relation to this school? What are key values that guide my journey and behavior? What do I love most to do? How am I authentic? How am I accountable (and to whom)? Or, consider mentoring expert Bob Biehl's helpful activity: "If you could stand on a platform for fifteen minutes talking to every person alive, what would you tell them? This helps you focus on your life message."

4. Possess and practice Christlike discipline. Remember that the core of discipline is "disciple," which means to follow, to learn, to shape, and to grow.

5. Ask for, receive, and use God's wisdom (Luke 12:11–12). You might question, for example, whether or not you should teach in a secular school hostile to the Christian faith. Never be afraid to prayerfully explore other options. God always opens and closes doors. His timing is *always* perfect. Our challenge is to discern his will for our lives and obey.

6. Develop a biblical view of the situation you are dealing with. You are the adult in your teaching relationships with students. God knows exactly what you are doing and what your motivation for doing something is. Be a positive, forgiving, and non-judgmental cheerleader. Always follow the example of Jesus. He made the greatest sacrifice on the cross. He selflessly surrendered his life for you and me to point the pathway to forgiveness and salvation. You might be called to share in his suffering and in his glory (Rom 8:17). Are you willing?

> Paul focused his life on Jesus Christ's idea of a New Testament saint; that is, not one who merely proclaims the gospel, but one who becomes broken bread and poured-out wine in the hands of Jesus Christ for the sake of others. (Oswald Chambers) [1]

7. Always walk in love (1 Cor 16:13). Consistently and continually pray for others, as Jesus modeled to his disciples. Help and encourage others to become the best people God created them to be using their unique gifts and talents to fulfill his greater purpose.

Reflect on this question: If the whole world followed me, would it be a better world?

Learn from the lives of others

When we study the lives of biblical characters like Moses, David, Rahab the prostitute, Elijah, Ruth, and the apostles Paul and Peter, we observe how God calls ordinary men and women, all of whom were sinners forgiven by him, to undertake his extraordinary work in a variety of settings. The stories of the movers and shakers at the end of each chapter remind us that God, as modeled by Jesus, always equips and empowers those he calls to be his hands, feet, and voice in a broken world (Prov 16:3; 18:10; 1 Tim 1:12–17).

---

1. Reimann, *My Utmost for His Highest*, February 25.

Sharon had a heart for serving others. Sometimes she was misunderstood and felt that a couple of her line managers neither supported nor trusted her. Eventually she felt God call her to move on. She wrote me a note: "I do wish to thank you for all your support, encouragement, listening ears, and prayers over my time at [the school]. Thank you for helping me through my disappointments, times of discouragement, and rejection and for being God's light . . . Thank you for always seeing the best in me . . . listening to my gripes and for having confidence in me. Mostly I want to thank you for making me feel like I belonged when so often I felt as though I didn't."

Protection from Satan's daily attacks

How do you protect yourself from Satan's daily deceptive strategies?

We cannot always expect to be liked and admired as we strive to become like Jesus. We can prepare ourselves for rejection and ridicule. Paul shared with Timothy this harsh reality of Christian ministry: "In fact, everyone who wants to live a godly life in Christ Jesus will be persecuted" (2 Tim 3:12).

Paul wrote to the Ephesians while sitting chained to a Roman soldier. His crime was that he preached the gospel in obedience to God's call on his life.

Paul's workplace, similar to that of most teachers, was an opportunity for non-believers to see Jesus by observing Paul in action (Titus 2:6–10).

Teachers set a positive example when they show patience, perseverance, wisdom, and discernment when under attack from non-Christians; respond in a non-judgmental and loving way to an unfair or unjust comment, or express authentic forgiveness to someone who has wronged them.

Paul reminded the Ephesians that sin and Satan are the real enemies, *not* the people. These words remain relevant as we face our daily challenges.

Wear the armor of God every day

Paul offers a constructive strategy to stand firm against our spiritual enemies as we work towards positively transforming the lives of others: "Put on the full armor of God, so that you can take your stand against the devil's schemes" (Eph 6:11).

He describes an armor made up entirely of the spiritual weapons of truth, justice or righteousness, the good news (the gospel of peace), faith, God's saving power of salvation, God's message, and praying in the Spirit (Eph 6:10–18).

We prepare ourselves because we know that Satan is active and will do everything possible to undermine our work and our efforts to be a Christlike influence.

I experienced such challenges as a school principal in a secular school:

- A disgruntled parent accused me of racism. Disciplinary procedures were being discussed linked to her child's serious breach of the school's code of conduct.

- Another colleague at the same school publicly berated me and told untruths about my role in encouraging him to resign his position as a result of ongoing questionable behavior.

- I had the difficult task to retrench two colleagues when the school board decided to restructure an administrative area of the school.

I had another challenging task in a Christian school where I was the principal. I sensitively urged an under-performing teacher to move on after he had unsuccessfully received professional support and encouragement from a member of the senior leadership team. Fortunately, this colleague acknowledged that he would be happier in a tertiary environment.

In all these situations I wore God's armor every day as I prayed for wisdom and discernment beyond my years so I could respond compassionately to the challenges. I also consulted other colleagues and board members.

The Bible encourages us never to cease praying and to prioritize looking after our personal health and wellbeing if we wish to be positive members of our community.

Mary Yerkes author and a certified spiritual director stresses the importance of a balanced lifestyle:

> Balanced living is healthy living. It is Christ-centered and encompasses the whole of who we are—spirit, soul and body. A balanced life enables us to enter fully into God's plan and purpose for us in each season of life, stretching, yet honoring our physical, mental, and emotional capacities and limits.[2]

A healthy and balanced lifestyle

How do you care for your health and wellbeing?

A spiritually healthy and balanced lifestyle enables you to face your daily challenges with self-belief and confidence, as non-teaching staff member Sue demonstrated in her mentoring relationship with fifteen-year-old Liam.

Sue a committed Christian had received extensive mentor training prior to mentoring Liam. Her passion was to work alongside young people and encourage them to reach their potential. She placed her family needs first, did not over-commit herself, exercised regularly and willingly asked for support when this was needed.

Liam was in serious trouble at school when he met Sue. Nine months later, at a function to celebrate the mentoring program, Liam publicly acknowledged Sue:

> Thank you for all the help and support you have given me over the months we have been together. You have made me realize that nothing is impossible and I can be anything I aspire to be.
>
> You've made me stronger both physically and mentally. Before I met you, my anger got the best of me. Now, through your support, anger and depression no longer

2. Yerkes, *A Christ-Centered Model*, 3.

are a part of me. Now I believe in making something of my life and to better my future. You have shown me the importance of a good career and the benefits of a healthy lifestyle.

I could never thank you enough. You were truly the most caring person I've ever met. And I wish to thank you for your commitment to me. You've made me a better person and for that I'll never forget you. Thank you.

Ten years later Liam had completed his tertiary education and was pursuing a successful career. Sue remained the wise guide on the side.

Seven key strategies for modeling a balanced, Christlike lifestyle

Consider this checklist of possible strategies, which deliberately overlaps with the seven key strategies to place Jesus as Lord of our lives covered earlier in this chapter:

1. Spend time each day reading the Bible, meditating on its teaching and praying. Develop and nurture relationships with others who share your faith. As examples, consider involvement in a church fellowship group, or a church outreach program, or praise and worship activities, or some other faith-related program.

2. Care for yourself physically through regular exercise—a brisk thirty-minute walk each day, for example—a healthy diet, and having sufficient sleep. Researchers recommend between seven and nine hours sleep each night. Plan your diet, eat more vegetables, and have a healthy breakfast. Limit the use of alcohol and other substances. Never rely on these substances for relaxation, or to escape personal or work challenges. Develop strategies to positively monitor and manage your stress. For example, undertake a breathing exercise or a Christian meditative activity, or follow relaxation techniques and other physical or cultural activities you enjoy.

3. Foster and maintain your close personal relationships with family and trusted friends. It is important to sustain and keep Christian friends.

4. Discipline yourself to create the right balance between your professional role and your personal life. Find a trusted mentor, your non-judgmental cheerleader, to guide your personal and professional growth, and pray regularly for and with you.

5. Manage your finances responsibly to avoid potentially stressful situations that could negatively impact your teaching role.

6. Make time for fun, relaxing and mentally enriching activities. Puzzles, crosswords, singing, playing a musical instrument, painting, and drama are examples of activities for healthy living and positive brain development.

7. Pursue hobbies and interests with friends, preferably away from your work environment.

Prayerfully reflect on these strategies. Is there one strategy God wants you to work on now? Remember that the Christian journey is life-long. Be patient with yourself.

MOVERS AND SHAKERS

God calls different people at different times. He shapes, refines and showers them with his unconditional love and grace. Then he sends them out to positively impact the global community, often at great personal cost. Jackie Pullinger and Brother Andrew give meaning to American poet Theodore Roethke's challenge: "What we need are more people who specialize in the impossible."

Jackie Pullinger (1944–), as a young woman, was called by God to set out from England to do his work. She ended up with a ministry in the Kowloon Walled City in Hong Kong, where she worked with young people and focused on drug rehabilitation and evangelism. Jackie eventually established St Stephen's Society. This global ministry brings hope to the hopeless, often at great personal cost, and involves overcoming numerous obstacles. Jackie wrote the acclaimed book *Chasing the Dragon*, which describes her experiences in Hong Kong.

> God wants us to have soft hearts and hard feet. The trouble with so many of us is that we have hard hearts and soft feet. (Jackie Pullinger)

Brother Andrew (1928–), founder of Open Doors, is a Christian missionary born in the Netherlands. His real name is Andrew van der Bijl. Andrew gained international acclaim for the work he undertook, at great personal cost, smuggling Bibles to communist countries during the Cold War (1947–1991). He earned the nickname "God's Smuggler," which is also the title of the book about his life. Later he extended this ministry to the Middle East. Andrew's father was deaf and his mother a semi-invalid. One of six children, he led an adventurous and wild life. He entered the Dutch Army aged eighteen. He continued with his reckless lifestyle until he was shot in the ankle and hospitalized when he was twenty-four. The Franciscan sisters, who nursed him, radiated joyful servanthood. This had a deep impact on Andrew and resulted in him reading the Bible and later giving his life to God.

> Through prayer we can reach into the future and with loving hands touch those beyond our reach. (Brother Andrew)

SUCCESS

Success is speaking words of praise,
In cheering other people's ways,
In doing just the best you can,
With every task and every plan.
It's silence when your speech would hurt,
Politeness when your neighbor's curt.
It's loyalty when duty calls,
It's courage when disaster falls,
It's patience when the hours are long,
It's found in laughter and in song,
It's in the silent time of prayer,
In happiness and in despair.
In all of life and nothing less,
We find the thing we call Success.

—AUTHOR UNKNOWN

When God measures a person, there is a tape around the
heart, not the head.

—AUTHOR UNKNOWN

CHAPTER 3

Empowerment

Tell me and I forget. Teach me and I remember.
Involve me and I learn.

—BENJAMIN FRANKLIN, FOUNDING FATHER OF THE
UNITED STATES

REFLECTION

REFLECT ON YOUR DAY. Ask God to highlight something he believes is important in your day—an interaction with a student, parent or colleague; a "wow!" moment; a positive breakthrough; a positive or negative feeling; something relatively minor yet important to you. Pray about this from your heart in God's presence. Invite him to continue empowering you as his ambassador in your community.

PRACTICAL STRATEGIES

How effectively do you give students the space to decide, and the authority, or freedom to make choices? What age-appropriate teaching strategies do you use?

Jesus is the master teacher, indeed the greatest teacher of all time. He was called "teacher" sixty-six of the ninety times he was addressed directly in the gospels.

> He was the greatest teacher our world has ever known and most morally incisive preacher ever to grace our planet's life. (Dr Michael Cassidy)[1]

> You call me 'Teacher' and 'Lord,' and rightly so, for that is what I am (John 13:13).

It could be argued that the entire ministry of Jesus focused on empowering people to use their God-given gifts and talents to fulfill his greater purpose. When we feel empowered, we accomplish more than we initially thought possible. We have the freedom and authority to make choices.

Jesus modeled how compassionate authority encourages, draws out hidden gifts and talents, and enables great things to happen as he interacted with a variety of people (Prov 22:6, 1 Pet 4:10). He also modeled how people with good character remain vulnerable as they extend their hearts to touch the hearts of others.

Understand character

Our character, an important component of empowerment, is essentially the abilities we need to meet the demands of our teaching careers as transformers in our communities. In the Greek language, "character" means our experiences. It refers to our internal makeup, which naturally includes our relationships and connections with others. It is an awareness of our strengths and weaknesses, our ability to take control of our lives, set personal goals, and have the self-confidence and self-belief to make positive choices.

Colleagues, students and their families follow teachers because of their character and the integrity of their lives—teachers they respect and trust; teachers who are authentic, admired, and who treat others fairly and equally no matter what position they hold; teachers who empower as they allow others the authority and freedom to do something.

---

1. Cassidy, *Chasing the Wind*, 108

Author Napoleon Hill offers some useful guidance: "Sow an act, and you reap a habit. Sow a habit, and you reap a character. Sow a character, and you reap a destiny."

Vicky was a colleague who experienced difficult times with some colleagues, while also dealing with challenging personal issues. We spent time building a relationship of mutual respect and trust. We explored her relationship and communication skills. We identified her strengths and weaknesses, and discussed ways to use her gifts and talents more effectively. She tried different strategies and evaluated them with me on a regular basis. She improved her planning, organization, and management of time skills. Vicky wrote: "I would just like to say thanks for all the guidance during the past four-and-a-half years. Thanks for believing in me and encouraging me to be the best that I could be. Thank you for sharing in the many tough times in my life and at [school] and helping me to go smoother. I didn't think I would ever say this—but thanks for challenging me not only at work but also in my journey with God."

I spoke to the potential Vicky struggled to see. Vicky took control of her life during this self-empowering journey, grew in her Christian faith and worked at making positive choices. This season of Vicky's life encouraged her to undertake further study and follow a passion which had been crushed by others while she raised a young family. She eventually launched an incredible ministry focused on empowering people experiencing significant psychological and physical challenges.

Eight important qualities of transformative teachers

Personal empowerment involves a deeper understanding and awareness of oneself as a unique character called by God for a specific purpose. This will involve daily Bible reading, reflection, discussions with the special people in your life, and prayer.

This lifelong journey will inevitably have high and low moments.

Reflect on the following qualities of empowering and transformative teachers to develop a healthy mindset:

1. Vision—able to see into the future. Have a clear, exciting idea, rubber-stamped by God, of where they are going and what they want to accomplish, which is aligned with their values. They set some benchmarks and a framework within which to work. They can succinctly communicate a vision. They offer a hopeful future, as students are keen to learn from teachers and influential people who are visionaries. They can discuss the "hero" figures in their students' lives to gain insights into the values and beliefs of these young people, and help them attain *their* life visions.

2. Courage—willing to take calculated, non-life-threatening risks with no assurance of success. The word courage comes from the Latin word "cor," which means "heart"; a courageous life is a life lived from the center, a deeply rooted life. Courageous teachers have the strength of character to act upon what is best for the school and their work environment. This includes, on occasions, being proactive and discouraging life-threatening behavior.

3. Integrity—truthful at all times. Develop strong relationships built on trust. "Integrity is the core of our character. Without integrity we have a weak foundation upon which to build other Christ-like characteristics." (L. Lionel Kendrick, teacher)

4. Humility—able to acknowledge mistakes and be vulnerable, while remaining strong and decisive; able to contain their ego. "Humility is having the self-confidence and self-awareness to recognize the value of others without feeling threatened." (Brian Tracy, author)

5. Focus—able to focus on their strengths and the strengths of others; to focus on what must be achieved; able to challenge students to move out of their comfort zones, yet not out of strength zones; able to encourage others to set goals and chase dreams that are aligned with their values and feelings. "You are one decision away from living the life of your dreams! If you don't like what's going on in your life, you can

make the decision to change. When you change, everything else adjusts to accommodate that change." (Dr Cindy Trimm, Christian life coach)

6. Plan—able to strategize and be proactive, well-organized, with good management of time skills.

7. Patience and persistence—not a quitter. Appreciate that those they interact with will learn at a different pace.

8. Collaboration—able to work with others, yet speak effectively and persuasively, while respectfully asking tough questions.

Transformative teachers understand that empowerment is important for a happy, successful, and peaceful life (Luke 13:13, John 1:12–13). God strengthens us with a power that the world cannot receive and many do not understand. We are urged not to compare ourselves to the world or to be of the world: "But you are a chosen people, a royal priesthood, a holy nation, God's special possession, that you may declare the praises of him who called you out of darkness into his wonderful light." (1 Pet 2:9)

The spiritually empowering learning environment

How do visitors to your classroom feel and experience the spiritually empowering atmosphere?

Teachers undertake a variety of roles during this empowering journey. Students in our classrooms:

- Actively involve themselves in co-creating tasks and projects with each other by their actions and words.

- Learn how to mentally process the steps involved in solving a problem.

- Connect with us and with one another in an enriching, age-appropriate, safe student-centered environment (see Appendix 2).

Other examples might include learning situations in which we:

- Appear animated, and authentically responsive to our students' needs. Learning occurs when the developing brain is actively engaged.

- Create opportunities for students to connect regularly with their peers and with us. Examples might include laughter, non-threatening physical activities, acting kindly, collaboratively solving a puzzle, enjoying brain breaks during lessons, accomplishing a task, or eating a favorite food. These moments increase the dopamine levels and are important in the positive brain development of young people.

  > Brain breaks are brief physical activities involving collaboration and fun that provide a five-minute break from sitting down and formal learning . . . improve class engagement . . . reduce disruptive behavior and improve the focus and social behavior of the students. (Dr Helen Street)[2]

- Model courtesy and respect to our students, so they learn the importance of these vital character qualities in the development of meaningful relationships.

- Model the importance of having a moral compass to guide one's life and ethical choices, teaching students that *why* they act is as important as *how* they act.

We are engaged in important work as we encourage our students' creativity, innovative and entrepreneurial thinking. Most students, especially during adolescence, enjoy diversity and desire change.

Our students know that they are expected to succeed because they connect with us and trust us. They are aware that we care for them as unique individuals when we acknowledge their *efforts* rather than levels of intelligence. Pula shared about her math teacher Lindsay many years after leaving school: "I know I was blessed to have Mrs. R for math. Her teaching style and ability to understand a diverse group of students kept me engaged, focused,

2. Street, *Contextual Wellbeing*, 49.

and never ever wanting to miss a class. I will never ever forget the first time she let me stand up and write on the board what I thought was the solution to an equation. She beamed with pride and said, "That's it, excellent!" Because of you, ma'am, I kicked that final . . . exam and got a B!"

Set high standards to nurture empowerment

Realistic yet high standards are set. Clear rules and guidelines for effective and meaningful classroom learning are in place. Boys, especially, appreciate learning in such environments.

We teach students the importance of being accountable for the choices they make.

We coach students how to pause and think before they speak or act. Practice improves a student's skills, changes their brain, and builds its capacity to use these skills.

We model how to be an effective listener and how to use positive body language as we communicate with students.

We create an atmosphere in which everyone is committed to nurturing each other's highest sense of self by acting with kindness, care and respect. Neuroscience studies show that when students are in a positive emotional condition, they remember more of what they hear and read.

The importance of setting goals

These teaching methods and skills are especially important for empowering students living in difficult circumstances or high-risk environments. These students need social support and to understand that their lives have meaning and purpose. We teach these students the power to set goals and chase their dreams when we focus on their efforts and strengths, one small task at a time, and treat them with dignity and respect (1 Cor 15:58, 2 Tim 4:2).

This was evident when I spent about a year working with William, a talented sportsman with a challenging home life. He was underperforming academically. He approached me to assist him attain a sport scholarship, a long-term ambition. We had a number of tough, heart-to-heart conversations, working out how he could develop his strengths and focus on his studies. He wrote me this note a couple of months before he finished his schooling: "No words can express my gratitude towards you for all your help this year. I honestly don't think I could have done it without you."

William gained a lucrative sport scholarship the following year, allowing him to chase his dream of becoming a professional sportsman.

Transformative teachers continually look for new, more effective and empowering ways to teach. They appreciate the importance of educating students to play constructive roles in a fast-changing global community. These teachers attend courses, workshops, conferences, visit the classrooms of teaching colleagues, share and develop resources with colleagues, read relevant articles or books, listen to education podcasts, or watch encouraging and informative video-clips. They are teachable.

Use our God-given gifts to empower others

How do you measure your level of success empowering your students?

God measures our success not by what we *have*, but by what we *do* with what we have—how we use our gifts and talents—because everything is a gift from him for his glory and for service to others.

Jesus had the ability to teach in a direct and clear way. He used stories or parables to point people to the truth of his message. We can undertake the same empowering role, no matter what teaching environment we are in, as most students love stories.

The parables of the bags of gold (or talents) (Matt 25:14–30) and the ten minas (Luke 19:11–27), remind us that we are managers to whom God has entrusted resources and responsibilities until Jesus returns. These resources include our skills, jobs, time, wealth, mental capacities, and physical bodies. Eventually we will give God a full account of how we have used these resources (Luke 19:15).

Naledi wrote a note to her teacher Aiden some years after she left school. She acknowledged the empowering role Aiden had undertaken during a confusing time in her life: "Thank you for understanding my crazy enough life to help me figure out what I needed to study beyond secondary school. I always tell people that I was privileged to have someone who could put it all together. Even my parents had no idea how to define my potential and translate my grades, passion, and natural talent into a field of study. We just didn't. Your expertise and knowledge of what was being offered at tertiary level set a solid foundation for everything that I do today."

Reflect on how effectively you encourage students on their personally chosen pathways—my way is not the only way; this is not for my glory but for my students' success. Celebrate and support faltering steps to that independence. Picture a child learning to ride a bike. You allow them to wobble and eventually fall. You help them up and accompany them all the way to independence. We hope and pray that, ultimately, these young people will become positive members of an *interdependent* community.

The key Christian empowering quality: faithfulness

How do you honor and obey God with whatever he has given you?

The key quality Jesus looks for is faithfulness, as expressed in the parable of the bags of gold (or talents): "His master replied, 'Well done, good and faithful servant! You have been faithful with a few things'" (Matt 25:21).

How faithfully we serve God with what he has entrusted to us is more important than wealth, prestige, power, or fame (Ps 86:11–13, Rom 8:14–17).

We are encouraged to remain in touch with our true spiritual selves. Sometimes we feel overwhelmed, helpless, frustrated, or go through a wilderness experience. We wonder where God is. We might want to quit. We might experience ongoing tension with a colleague or parent. We might struggle with a student displaying persistent antisocial behavior tendencies. We might feel overwhelmed by the demands on our time during a busy period of a term. As a school principal, we might experience a sense of loneliness while grappling with a highly confidential situation.

During these times God calls us to greater faithfulness, and invites us into deeper intimacy with him (Deut 8:1–3). Jesus experienced this in the wilderness when he was tempted by Satan. He stayed focused on God and did not fall into the traps of instant gratification and entitlement (Luke 4:1–13).

How to respond to setbacks in an empowering way

Character is seen in how we respond to failure and setbacks. Do you acknowledge failure and admit you will never be perfect? Do you blame others or make excuses?

We deliberately pause during challenging times, and allow ourselves to enter the same intimate, fearless, and empowering relationship with God, "Abba," that Jesus experienced (Rom 8:15, Gal 4:6). The Spirit of Jesus reminds us that God's unconditional love and grace embraces and nurtures us. God provides us with the inner strength to persevere and overcome the inevitable obstacles that confront us. He provides the power as long as we remain willing (Luke 21:33). God coaches us to understand how, ultimately, he does the empowering work. We are merely his players carrying out his goals for our lives to achieve his purpose.

This is a "power-full" relationship. As we learn to sow the seeds of optimistic thinking into our lives, we develop an expectation that, no matter what situation we are in, things *will* get better because God is good (Heb 12:1–13, Jas 3:17–18).

Parents as partners during the empowering journey

How do you involve parents in meaningful ways in their children's self-discovery and self-empowerment journey?

Great teachers encourage students to embark on this holistic journey and regard parents as partners, not adversaries. Educator Rita Pierson highlights the importance of a significant adult in the life of a young person: "Every child deserves a champion—an adult who will never give up on them, who understands the power of connection, and insists that they become the best they can possibly be."

Benjamin was a member of a hockey team I coached. He made a poor choice that resulted in his departure from the school. This was a difficult time for the family. I met with Benjamin a few times to discuss his feelings and explore his future options. On some days he wanted to quit. On other days he was angry and frustrated about what had happened. On other days he felt ready to move on. A couple of months after his departure, his mother wrote to me: "Thank you for being such an understanding friend to Benjamin and a support to us. When we hit rock bottom it was good to know that there is a friend who cares. We can only move forward now and help and encourage Benjamin to become a man. We are giving him all the love and support that we can, although we do feel inadequate at times. This is where we really appreciate your love and understanding for Benjamin."

Benjamin learned from his experience, settled in a new school, and made good progress. He experienced a self-empowering journey, learned about the consequences of his choices, identified some of his strengths and positive character qualities, and ultimately realized the importance of not succumbing to negative peer pressure.

Seven key empowering strategies

This checklist of seven empowering strategies can be adapted to different age groups and embraces a positive partnership with parents.

1. Appreciate the different physical and emotional developmental journeys of girls and boys. Every word, action, and

facial expression—a smile, a nod of the head—is interpreted in a positive or negative manner by your perceptive students. It is only in the later teenage years that their brains are sufficiently developed to enable students to fully understand facial expressions.

2. Negotiate high yet achievable goals with your students, and provide support to help them reach these personal goals. Your words can change lives, intrinsically motivate, and empower. "How are you feeling about . . . ?" "I bet you are feeling pretty good about . . ." Discuss goal setting and the effective management of time with your students. Model these characteristics yourself. Sometimes goal setting is a positive way to connect with and affirm students, and learn something about their values. It enhances the development of the brain's executive function skills (planning, organizing, selecting, and learning strategies), especially during adolescence. Have realistic expectations. Focus on your students' performance and efforts, not just the outcomes, as you guide them to develop lifelong competencies.

3. Offer an experiential learning journey that most students enjoy. They learn best by doing (self-discovery) as they have little fear of change, and are learning how to make choices in a safe and secure environment.

4. Students tend to value learning from authentic older people they respect, and who walk the talk. These people explain the relevance of the subject a student is studying. They offer diverse learning experiences and activities to cater for different learning styles. While planning, ask yourself questions like: What important skills or knowledge are the students learning in this lesson? How do the activities I am planning intrinsically motivate, and inspire student learning? How is this lesson or activity empowering the students? How positively am I involving parents in their children's education?

5. Always offer constructive, concise and clear feedback, which students appreciate. Use empowering rather than judgmental

phrases. "You are not producing your best work yet." ("Yet" contains the message that, with greater effort, new strategies, or other levels of support, progress will be made.) "You are awesome!" "Your effort was amazing—well done! I am so proud of you." "You are generous."

6. Promote a spirit of enterprise and initiative among your students, identifying and naming strengths. Teach students how to use their strengths to take an idea and translate it into a product. You are enhancing their resiliency.

7. Teach students important, age-appropriate skills to enhance the growth mindset: how to prioritize, plan, and effectively manage their time; how to develop their analytical skills; how to manage impulses and feelings; how to look at themselves positively and create supportive networks around themselves; how to switch or sustain attention; how to solve a problem; how to stick to a plan, and how to assess risk. Andrew Fuller points out that the brain is not wired for multitasking:

> When students are distracted and multitasking, the neural circuitry that underpins learning a new concept is often not formed. On average it takes 400 percent longer to learn the same amount of information when you multitask and the likelihood that you learn it patchily increases. [3]

MOVERS AND SHAKERS

God calls us to serve him with our gifts and talents. He empowers us with the skills, inner strength, and intrinsic motivation to undertake his work. He does not promise an easy journey, though always assures us we are never alone, as the lives of Mother Teresa of Calcutta and John Wesley attest.

Mother Teresa of Calcutta (1910–1997) was an Albanian-Indian Roman Catholic nun and missionary. She was born in Skopje, Macedonia, and her mother had a strong and positive influence on

---

3. Fuller, *Re-inventing schools*, 4

her faith journey. Mother Teresa was one of the Sisters of Loreto until, called, equipped, and empowered by God, she established the Missionary of Charity in India and spent the rest of her life serving the poorest of the poor. In 1979 she was awarded the Nobel Peace Prize. Always a controversial figure, she left a legacy that continues to reach out to the marginalized people in society.

> Spread love everywhere you go. Let no one ever come to you without leaving happier . . . If you judge people, you have no time to love them. (Mother Teresa)

John Wesley (1703–1791), his brother Charles (who wrote 6,000 hymns), and fellow cleric George Whitefield founded Methodism (the Methodist church). John was heavily influenced by his parents. The courage and commitment John displayed as he traveled across Great Britain and Ireland helping to organize and form small Christian groups is a fascinating story of trust and faith in God. During the eighteenth century many Methodists became influential and empowered leaders of globally significant social issues such as prison reform and the abolition of slavery.

> Do all the good you can, by all the means you can, in all the ways you can, at all the times you can, to all the people you can, as long as ever you can. (John Wesley)

UNITY

I dreamed I stood in a studio
And watched two sculptors there.
The clay they used was a young child's mind,
And they fashioned it with care.
One was a teacher. The tools he used
Were books, and music, and art.
One parent with a guiding hand,
And a gentle, loving heart.
Day after day, the teacher toiled,
With touch that was deft and sure.
While the parents labored by his side
And polished and smoothed it o'er.
And when at last their task was done,
They were proud of what they wrought.
For this thing they had molded in the child
Could neither be sold nor bought.
And each agreed he would have failed
If he had worked alone.
For behind the parent stood the school
And beside the teacher the home.
—AUTHOR UNKNOWN

The object of education is to prepare the young to educate
themselves throughout their lives.
—ROBERT M. HUTCHINS,
EDUCATIONAL PHILOSOPHER

CHAPTER 4

Empathy

A gentle person treads lightly, listens carefully, looks tenderly and touches with reverence.

—HENRI NOUWEN, THEOLOGIAN

REFLECTION

REFLECT ON YOUR DAY. Where did you specifically find God in your teaching experience today? In God's presence, focus on that moment or those moments. What feelings did you experience? What gift or gifts did you use? Allow these thoughts and feelings to turn into prayer and thank God for using you as a transformative teacher today.

PRACTICAL STRATEGIES

How well do you know the students, their parents, and the colleagues you interact with on a daily basis? Can you remember one colleague, student, or parent you reached out to in a positive and encouraging way today?

Empathetic teachers try their best to understand how another person is feeling by walking in that person's shoes for a while.

Jesus modeled the power of empathetic authority in his interactions with people, and lived out his instruction to the Pharisees:

"Love the Lord your God with all your heart and with all your soul and with all your mind. This is the first and greatest commandment. And the second is like it: Love your neighbor as yourself" (Matt 22:37–39).

Jesus showed empathy when he expressed compassion to the crowds: "When he saw the crowds, he had compassion on them, because they were harassed and helpless, like sheep without a shepherd" (Matt 9:36).

Jesus showed empathy when he expressed compassion to the widow before raising her son from death to life: "When the Lord saw her, his heart went out to her and he said, 'Don't cry'" (Luke 7:11).

Jesus showed empathy when he expressed compassion towards Martha and Mary, the sisters of Lazarus: "Jesus wept" (John 11:35). He felt their hurt and pain. This showed how much he cared. He proceeded to raise Lazarus from the dead.

These examples of the life and ministry of Jesus encourage us to develop our capacity to *feel* other people's emotional states, attitudes, and thoughts, and to identify the emotional states in both ourselves and others (Rom 12:15; 1 Pet 3:8). We use these emotions to effectively facilitate thinking and behavior as empathetic teachers.

Be the heart of Jesus

We are never expected to fix families or rescue children. However, when we are the heart of Jesus we feel and share others' pain or joy. We are present in the lives of others. We do our best to emotionally understand and share their experiences and feelings.

We are effective teachers when we contribute to the creation of a caring, trusting, and transparent culture in our work environment. Our students move ahead one step at a time, often at a different pace. We display an empathetic attitude, and acknowledge their uniqueness.

The parable of the good Samaritan (Luke 10:25–37) encourages us to reach out to members of our school community as non-judgmental cheerleaders. We remove any prejudices and model how to follow the command of Jesus: "Love your neighbor as yourself" (Luke 10:27), a love that knows no boundaries.

The parable explores issues such as racial and ethnic divisions, violent crime, and cross-cultural relationships. The Samaritan does not fix or eliminate these issues. He displays a refreshingly open and courageous attitude to the scene that confronts him on the road to Jericho. He reaches out empathetically, as an agent of mercy, to a man in pain who belongs to a member of a faction his faith group loathed.

Open to change

How open are you to change teaching ideas and methodology? Do you display an empathetic attitude towards those who lead or facilitate important changes in your school environment? How open are you to change your thinking as a result of the feedback or new ideas your students share with you?

Empathetic and skilled teachers look for the opportunities to change things for the better. This journey takes time and years of experience, and usually involves some calculated risks. These teachers are bold, patient, and prefer a constructive team environment.

We learn to identify the best approach and make the changes happen. This may be through supporting a new way of doing things because we have an open mind and are teachable, or through a new process or structure, or through transforming an old model of teaching. We make changes with an empathetic attitude and respect the reactions of others during this process.

Our lives are a reflection of Jesus (Rom 13:14) when we walk closely with God. The Holy Spirit guides our thoughts and speech: "Do not worry about how you will defend yourselves or what you will say, for the Holy Spirit will teach you at that time what you should say" (Luke 12:11–12). Experienced educator and former school principal Dr Marion Sanders wrote about lessons she learned over the years:

Obeying God's directions changed my focus from fear to hope, inadequacy to confidence, from noticing deficits to celebrating strengths, and from distaste to delight.[1]

Be the clay in the hands of the potter

Yet you, Lord, are our Father.
We are the clay, you are the potter,
we are all the work of your hand (Isa 64:8).

We invite God to freely use us, the clay, in any way he wants.

Then the word of the Lord came to me. He said, "Can I not do with you, Israel, as this potter does?" declares the Lord. "Like clay in the hand of the potter, so are you in my hand, Israel" (Jer 18:5–6).

We receive the security we value and cherish when we surrender ourselves to God's unconditional love. He empowers us, like the potter, to empathetically and compassionately break down, rebuild, mold, shape and refine the lives of those entrusted to our care. We become courageous game-changers in our communities.

Sally was a young teaching colleague with an ability to move alongside struggling students. Empathy, compassion, and creativity were three significant qualities she displayed on many occasions when working alongside students, parents, and colleagues—sometimes at great personal cost. The extracurricular, non-sporting activities she coordinated were always over-subscribed. Sally was a wonderful example of how to speak to the potential of students between the ages of five and eleven and, at the same time, to identify the gifts of even the most challenging colleagues and help them feel valued and appreciated. Her humble attitude and deep faith remain an encouragement and inspiration to many.

1. Sanders, *Memoirs*, 17

A tribute to an amazing teacher—show empathy

Pulitzer Prize-winning American journalist Clark R. Mollenhoff wrote a poem as a tribute both to his mother, who had taught for forty years, and to the teachers who had inspired him at a young age. May this poem inspire, encourage and motivate you, an amazing teacher, to be like the potter and co-create some beautiful and wonderful experiences for your students. Be prepared to walk in their shoes for a while, and even feel the blisters.

TEACHERS

You are the molders of their dreams.
The gods who build or crush their
young beliefs of right and wrong.
You are the spark that sets aflame
the poet's hand or lights the flame
in some great singer's song.
You are the gods of the young—the very young.
You are the guardian of a million dreams.
Your every smile or frown can heal or pierce a heart.
Yours are one hundred lives—one thousand lives.
Yours is the pride of loving them, the sorrow, too.
Your patient work, your touch, make you the god of hope
that fills their souls with dreams,
and makes those dreams come true.

Seven key strategies of an empathetic teacher

How will your students remember you? Will it be as someone who "taught" them a subject or more than one subject? Will it be as someone who was there when they needed you? Will it be as someone who did your best to understand their unique life stories? Will it be as someone who tried to stand in their cultural shoes to see how their culture views the community, and then assesses why and what this means in the school's cultural context?

We automatically create the conditions in which students want to learn when we empathetically engage with them. These strategies show students that we can adapt to their particular issues:

1. We ensure our students feel emotionally and physically safe and secure. They are active participants within an enriching environment that stimulates the neuroplasticity of the brain, which grows when young people are spontaneous and having fun. This stress-free atmosphere is challenging, encourages social interaction, and promotes personal development. It allows students opportunities to take responsibility for their choices and to learn that failure is okay when they produce their best effort.

2. We use a variety of instructional techniques to cater for different learning styles.

3. We promote the students' creativity. We ask them for assistance when needed. We are more effective teachers when we know our students. Lucas faced some learning issues, yet was competent with anything linked to technology. I always asked him for assistance when I had an issue with my laptop or some other technology device in class. Lucas became a more empowered and involved learner. He felt valued and appreciated. His class members always called on him to help me because they respected his talent.

4. Students respect our fair and consistent approach to discipline. We negotiate age-appropriate boundaries or a code of conduct with our students. Students, especially boys, appreciate clear rules, boundaries, and procedures to follow. We understand their difficulties, hesitations, and complexes with our empathetic attitudes. We objectively communicate an awareness of their thoughts and feelings to help them better understand themselves. "If I were in your position, I would feel the same way." "I want to thank you for taking

the time and having the courage to speak to me today." "If I understand you correctly, what you are saying is . . ." Fairness involves never labeling students and not having favorites. We do not allow the academically strong students to dominate discussions or class work. We never humiliate a student. We never harass students with reprimands. We have clear grading or marking procedures. We are willing to give students the benefit of the doubt.

5. We are conscious of our body language. We learn to look behind the outward appearances and show empathy. We know when to speak to a student's potential that he or she might be unable to see.

6. We remove the "but" from our sentences. When we replace "but" with "and," the statement is positive and appropriate.

7. We are empathetic and non-judgmental listeners. We say "please" and "thank you" as we model polite respect. Students respect us when we "lead with our ears," and display an attitude of listening with a view to having our minds changed. We listen for what is not being said. Attentive listening usually promotes empathy and connectedness. "So, what you are saying is that . . ." "I sense that you feel . . ." "Would you or could you tell me a little bit more about that?" "Is there anything else?" "What was that like for you?"

Sandy taught in both Christian and secular schools:

"I am walking in the park with my grandchildren. A stranger approaches us. "Morning, Mr K! How are you?" *He shakes my hand warmly.* "I am Tuma! You saved my life once!" Now I am surprised as no one has warmly suggested that teaching English has "saved" anyone's life. The story continues in choked excitement.

"I was a boy from [a high-risk environment] in your boarding house. A few boys had a rough and tumble in one of the dormitories and I pulled out a sharp instrument and struck out. Well, you handled the affair wonderfully. It stopped there and then. I never had anything else happen to me and I completed my schooling at [the school]. I am now an engineer with two children at [the school] and my moment of madness might have ended my 'life' as an academic right there if it had been differently handled! Thank you for saving my life!"

Sandy had the wisdom and experience to place the dormitory incident within the context of an apartheid South Africa transitioning to democracy. Schools were opening their doors to students of all races and cultures. Each student brought their unique life story into the school environment. Sandy's respectful and empathetic approach was acknowledged by Tuma all those years later.

> To listen another soul into a condition of disclosure and discovery may be almost the greatest service that any human being ever performed for another." (Dr Douglas Steele, clinical professor)

MOVERS AND SHAKERS

Sometimes other Christians reject our offers of service and leave us feeling perplexed. Yet, we persist in our search to serve God, and the door always opens at the appropriate time and in the right place. Gladys Aylward and Dwight L. Moody would have understood a comment someone once made: "The Christian life is not my responsibility, but my response to his ability."

Gladys Aylward (1902–1970) was a British Christian evangelist and missionary with an empathetic heart to serve the people of China. Gladys was raised an Anglican in a working-class family in North London. In her early teens, Gladys worked as a housemaid for a wealthy family, saving money to embark on missionary service. She felt God calling her to do his work in China. She settled in northern China in the early 1930s where she joined another Christian missionary, Jennie Lawson. They started an inn for mule drivers who were given food and rest and listened to Bible stories. In 1938 she led almost a hundred children, most between the ages of four and eight, on a one hundred miles journey over twenty-seven days to escape from Japanese invaders. This was made famous in the film *Inn of the Sixth Happiness*. She later returned to Taiwan where she established the Gladys Aylward Orphanage.

I have been a fisher of men. I went to China because God asked me. I did not have missionary training or missionary status. I was answerable to him and no one else. (Gladys Aylward)

Dwight L. Moody (1837–1899) was an empathetic American evangelist and publisher who experienced a tough upbringing. His father died when Dwight was only four years old, leaving the family in poverty. Dwight's mother strongly influenced his spiritual growth and guided him to seek God first and then his righteousness. As a young adult, Dwight moved from Massachusetts to Boston, where he worked in his uncle's shoe store. He attended the Congregational Church of Mount Vernon where he eventually converted and became a Christian evangelist, described by many as one of the greatest evangelists of the nineteenth century. The Great Chicago Fire in October 1871 destroyed Dwight's church, his family home, and the homes of many other church members. Dwight returned to his original home in Northfield, Massachusetts, where he purchased a farm. He ran Christian conferences and founded two schools that later merged into Northfield Mount Hermon School. Dwight traveled widely and shared the gospel message using his God-given gift of powerfully communicating the love of God.

Faith makes all things possible ... love makes all things easy." (D. L. Moody)

Strong sandaled feet that trod the earth at Galilee
Strong sandaled feet dusted with the sand of destiny
Brown strong feet creased with kneeling
While he washed the feet of others
Soothing sinews and souls . . . healing
Heels swung dust puffs from colt's hide
Palm fronds brush across his foot
People push, excited, sweaty
Do they really know whose feet these are?
Hosannas anyway
Strong sandaled feet chilled in the Garden
As he anguished in his human part
Then, as he knew, came blinding agony
Stakes of this world shattered strong brown feet
Freed at last, the essence flashed to former place
Yet in compassion leaves a part that we can know and love
Holy Spirit, companion, paracletus walk with us
Wash our feet and when we stumble hold us fast, we pray.
—BRIAN BROKENSHA, MD

How wonderful that nobody needs wait a single moment
before starting to improve the world.
—ANNE FRANK, DIARIST

CHAPTER 5

Humility

I am a little pencil in the hand of a writing God who is sending a love letter to the world.

—MOTHER TERESA

REFLECTION

REFLECT ON THE DAYS ahead and, in God's presence, ask him to give you light for the challenges you face. Focus on your feelings. Are you feeling enthused, apprehensive, filled with self-doubt, weary, fearful, or positively challenged? Turn these feelings into prayer. Is there a specific gift you might value for the days ahead? Encouragement, persistence, management of time, a sense of humor, patience, courage? Ask God to accompany you as you commit to serve him with humility to fulfill his greater purpose for your life.

PRACTICAL STRATEGIES

How challenging is it to remain humble as you strive to be a servant to others?

We appreciate our critical roles as teachers best—namely to serve others and be present in their lives, both for their and our own good—when we understand the importance of humility in the Christian walk.

Humble teachers take attention away from themselves and place it where it belongs, on others and for the greater good of their communities.

We appreciate that we are neither better than the people we are working with, nor more important, nor more worthy. Indeed, people are unlikely to trust us if they see that we are driven by pride, jealousy, ego ("Edge God Out"), or the belief that we are better than they are.

Jesus could have had everything he wanted—titles, status, self-centered power, and the acclamation of people. However, instead of self-promotion, and in obedience to God, he lowered himself to a position of serving others. This is the essence of a Christlike teacher (Luke 22:27).

One of the first thoughts of Jesus was how best to selflessly serve others as he carried out his Father's will. This came at great personal cost (Luke 9:23–24), something many Christian teachers, especially those working in secular environments, might experience.

Jesus modeled the importance of teaching and mentoring young people. Children loved to be with Jesus, as he was humble, gentle, and kind-hearted. And, he loved being in their presence (Matt 19:14, Mark 10:13–16, Luke 18:16).

Washing feet

Jesus longs for us to give ourselves to others in the same way that he gives himself to us: "For even the Son of Man did not come to be served, but to serve, and to give his life as a ransom for many" (Mark 10:45).

How can we do this?

Greg was principal of a school at which I taught. He attended the second day of the annual student leaders' camp held at the beginning of every year.

The morning began with a short service led by the chaplain, followed by breakfast. After breakfast Greg facilitated the first session of the day, during which he shared thoughts and ideas about servant leadership. He asked everyone to sit in a large circle before sharing the gospel account of Jesus washing his disciples' feet (John 13:1–17).

Greg proceeded to wash the feet of the school captains (head students). They, in turn, washed the feet of the student leader or teacher attending the camp sitting next to them and the foot washing moved around the circle. This was a time of silent and deep reflection. Participants had an opportunity to think about their roles as humble and positive people of influence. As student leaders, they were encouraged to serve others in a Christlike and empathetic way, working collaboratively and doing their best to obey the teaching of Jesus to his disciples after he had washed their feet: "I have set you an example that you should do as I have done for you. Very truly I tell you, no servant is greater than his master, nor is a messenger greater than the one who sent him. Now that you know these things, you will be blessed if you do them" (John 13:16–17).

Imagine each day, as we interact with students, that we are washing their feet. This includes the students who are cooperative, disruptive, back-chatting, bored and disinterested, grieving the loss of a loved one (including a pet), struggling to express feelings, highly motivated, disengaged, or disabled. We wash their feet just as Jesus washed the feet of the disciples. These disciples were ordinary people who undertook extraordinary work to spread the good news of the birth, life, death, resurrection, and ascension of Jesus to the wider community.

We teach students with the humble and empathetic attitude of Jesus. Higher levels of oxytocin, endorphins, dopamine, and other chemicals that give students a sense of wellbeing, safety, and belonging, are released in the brain when our daily narrative results in positive conversations with students and their families.

This is our daily ministry of modeling and pointing others to the unconditional love and grace of God. We will be amazed at how much we achieve when we grasp the truth that we are good enough to do what God has called us to do, and when we don't care who gets the credit. "Be completely humble and gentle; be patient, bearing with one another in love" (Eph 4:2).

Humble teachers take pride and joy in the achievements of their students when they focus on the students' wellbeing and development of intrinsic motivation (Jer 17:7–8). Students become unafraid to risk failure within the safe, age-appropriate environment teachers create. They learn to solve problems and ask questions. They are not afraid to share new ideas—even a variety of solutions to a problem—and, most importantly for the self-empowering journey, choose to take ownership of their learning.

The humble face of Jesus

What face do your students and colleagues see when they are in your presence? How does it reflect the face of the humble follower of Jesus?

"He guides the humble in what is right and teaches them his way" (Ps 25:9).

"Look to the Lord and his strength; seek his face always" (1 Chr 16:11).

The face of Jesus in the Beatitudes (Matt 5:3–12), explained in The Sermon on the Mount (Matt 5:1–7:29), portrays humility, gentleness, poverty, hunger, grief, a thirst for righteousness, compassion, and so much more. This self-portrait of Jesus reveals how we can be in the world without being of it. This is only possible when, with an open heart, we surrender our lives to him and humbly allow him to teach us the "right" actions of a "righteous," transformative teacher (Luke 6:19–23, John14:12, 15:15).

Then we can say, together with Paul: "I have been crucified with Christ and I no longer live, but Christ lives in me. The life I now live in the body, I live by faith in the Son of God, who loved me and gave himself for me" (Gal 2:20).

This is a lifelong journey as our imperfections open for us a vision of the perfect life that God, through Jesus, has promised us

(2 Cor 4:7–12). We continually remind ourselves to be patient and gentle with ourselves on this journey.

Often, we have no idea how our encouragement of others impacts their lives. I received this unexpected message from a colleague Penny:

> I just want to thank you from the bottom of my heart for the impact you have had on my life through your years at [the school]. You are a true man after God's own heart, kind, compassionate, patient, gentle, and understanding. I really have appreciated the times that you sat and listened to my concerns about my family and friends and the prayers that you have prayed for them and for me. You are an amazing person and I really do thank God for you. You have also greatly impacted the staff during our times in staff devotion. Thank you. That time has been such a blessing to us all. For me devotion has helped me to step out and be more confident about my own beliefs and to be able to share with others in a safe and comfortable environment, something I thought I couldn't do.

The importance of a forgiving heart

How do others see that you are faithful, available and teachable?

God sent Jesus to reconcile us with God and for us to reconcile people with one another (2 Cor 5:18–20). At no stage did he ever suggest this will be straightforward.

Sometimes we falter. We do or say something we later regret. We fail to carry out a task expected of us. We take our eyes off Jesus for a period of time and pursue our selfish ways.

When we humbly repent and are reconciled with God, we experience his forgiveness. We receive a new heart, new eyes to see, and new ears to hear (Luke 15:11–32). We experience freedom from the need to judge, or be a negative influence when we consult regularly with God and allow other Christians to embrace our lives.

Jesus looked at the disasters and the challenges of the world around him as opportunities to demonstrate God's unconditional love and grace. When we make ourselves fully available to God and obey him, he gives himself fully to us. Our challenge is to work faithfully when no one is watching (John 1:12, Eph 5:1–2, Col 3:12–14).

"Be kind and compassionate to one another, forgiving each other, just as in Christ God forgave you" (Eph 4:32).

Look at life through the eyes of Jesus

As we look at situations through the eyes of Jesus, we become reconcilers in our communities. We might also experience divisions, personality clashes, gossip, prejudice, and other secular influences that will continually challenge our faith.

We avoid comparing ourselves to others, as this leads to feelings of inadequacy, jealousy, envy, and insecurity. Instead, we strive to be teachers with integrity, always accountable for our choices and actions.

We learn how to offer a safe face and place for students and others when they feel vulnerable while dealing with challenging issues. They might live different lifestyles, not think, speak or act as we do, or are people who have hurt us (Luke 23:26–34; 1 John 2:15–17). We humbly remove the walls that separate.

Kieran was a talented and ambitious student, achieving strong academic results and actively engaged in the school's extra-curricular program. When he suffered some disappointments, he approached a teacher Ken for guidance. When Kieran completed his schooling, he wrote a note to Ken: "Thank you for your guidance over these last few years. You took the time out to sit down with me and explain things I can work on to develop myself as a member of the [school] community. I am incredibly grateful for the guidance you have given me, the continued lessons on humility . . . I most definitely grew as a person. Thank you for always being there for a chat. You have cemented yourself in my mind as a mentor, and I hope that next year with time permitting I can still come visit so I can pick your brain for new lessons to carry on into life."

Seven key strategies of a humble teacher

Practical tips of encouragement to be the humble face of Jesus:

1. Ask students, especially those who need personal encouragement, to help you with tasks like carrying workbooks (or the equivalent), cleaning the white board at the end of a lesson, or running errands as you show them how much they are valued and appreciated.

2. Encourage students and colleagues to evaluate your teaching and coaching. These actions show them that their ideas and opinions are valued and that you are humble and teachable.

3. Learn the age-appropriate language of your students. Take time to talk to them and find out more about them. Model humility in these moments. Remember that adolescents, especially, experience emotions before they can articulate them while the prefrontal cortex of the brain develops.

4. Facilitate an outreach project with students. This will teach them how to serve others with humility and not expect anything in return, other than the satisfaction of giving of themselves and their possessions to those in need.

5. Apologize when you know you have made an error of judgment. Prepare to be both vulnerable and accessible in your interactions with others.

6. Buy a cup of tea or coffee for a colleague in need of support and encouragement, or undertake some other random act of kindness, expecting nothing in return.

7. Care for someone marginalized by their peers or the community, or affected by an injustice.

> Because of the increase of wickedness, the love of most will grow cold, but the one who stands firm to the end will be saved. And this gospel of the kingdom will be preached in the whole world as a testimony to all nations, and then the end will come" (Matt 24:12–14).

We reach out our hands with an attitude of love. When we touch, we open windows and doors into our lives. We share emotions, experiences, and, most importantly, our hearts.

When we touch another's heart, the barriers collapse. We cross the bridge into another's life and allow that person to cross the bridge into our hearts.

I spent time with sixteen-year-old Mia. We exchanged thoughts and ideas about life issues and injustices that concerned her. My role was mostly to listen and clarify. Many months later she wrote: "It matters not what you are thought to be, but what you are. You have taught me that it is because of the walls we have built, that our people are lonely, and I promise to break down those walls and build bridges."

When we receive Mia's note, or a note like the following one I received from a colleague Dan we immediately give God all the glory and humbly thank him for how he has used us to touch another life. "I will miss my mentor, my friend, one of my inspirations and support and one of the greatest people I have ever had the privilege to work or journey with. My life is better for having you in it and I will be forever grateful that you helped me return to prayer and move closer to God again."

MOVERS AND SHAKERS

God blesses us with different gifts and talents. He uses them powerfully when we totally surrender our lives to him. The following stories demonstrate how God used two different personalities in life-changing ways during World War II. Their selflessness gives meaning to author Joy J. Golliver's belief that: "The meaning of life is to find your gift; the purpose of life is to give it away."

Corrie Ten Boom (1892–1983), a watchmaker, is well-known for the way her Dutch family—devout Christians—helped many Jews escape the Nazi Holocaust during World War II. She and her sister were sent to the Ravensbruck Concentration Camp, where her sister died. Her book, *The Hiding Place*, is an autobiography of her family's challenges during this difficult time. Corrie was known internationally as a humble ambassador of the power of forgiveness in Christ. She also set up rehabilitation centers to help Holocaust survivors.

> There is no panic in Heaven! God has no problems, only plans . . . Never be afraid to trust an unknown future to a known God. (Corrie Ten Boom)

Eric Liddell (1902–1945), "The Flying Scotsman," was an Olympic gold medal runner and Scottish international rugby union player. The son of missionaries, Eric's strong faith and humble ministry were championed in the film *Chariots of Fire*. Soon after the 1924 Summer Olympics in Paris, Eric returned to China as a missionary teacher. He was imprisoned in a Japanese civilian internment camp during World War II. He died there shortly before the war ended, though not before he had been the humble face of Jesus to many of those with whom he interacted, especially the children.

> We are all missionaries. Wherever we go we either bring people nearer to Christ or we repel them from Christ. (Eric Liddell)

A TEACHER'S MORNING PRAYER

O God, giver of the gift of life,
bless me this day as I go
to teach.
I thank you for my career,
and for the health and enthusiasm
you have given me.
I thank you for my students
and friends, in whose company
joys are doubled, sorrows soothed
and weakness changed into strength.
Help me to be cheerful today,
kind and loving to my students
that they may be happy in my company.

—AUTHOR UNKNOWN

A person with high self-efficacy believes they can reach their goal and they take the steps required to make it happen. They work harder. They raise their hands more. They ask questions. They practice, get it wrong and try again.

—CARMINE GALLO, AUTHOR

CHAPTER 6

Affirmation

The mediocre teacher tells. The good teacher explains. The superior teacher demonstrates. The great teacher inspires.
—WILLIAM A. WARD, PASTOR

REFLECTION

REFLECT ON YOUR DAY. Ask God to highlight moments when you affirmed a student, a group of students, a colleague or a parent. Visualize the moments and take ownership of your feelings during these times. Thank God for the way he used you to positively impact one or more lives. Invite him to equip you with more gifts to speak positively into the lives of others.

PRACTICAL STRATEGIES

How do you inspire and affirm students? How and when do you reach out and support your colleagues or the families of students?

We enter our work environments as followers of Jesus, and visible signs of God's unconditional love. People judge us not by what we say, but by how effectively we care and work at being humble, relational teachers (2 Tim 1:6–7). We appreciate the privilege of being God's affirming ambassadors. (Deut 32:2).

American psychiatrist William Glasser observed, "When you study great teachers . . . you will learn much more from their caring and hard work than from their style."

Dr Marion Sanders wrote about her experiences following Jesus in a variety of educational roles:

> My testimony is that God is present with us in our vocation. He speaks to us, and for us, in the midst of our daily tasks. He challenges our thinking and our decisions, and he actively intervenes to bring about his purposes when we are alert to his leading.[1]

A teacher's role involves imparting knowledge, guiding, and developing lifelong skills. We design and build value into our students' lives when we like and respect them. We use affirmations to create a positive and supportive community by teaching students to support one another. We connect with our students and colleagues when we genuinely affirm and intrinsically motivate them.

Connecting with our community

This connection is critically important, especially when working with students from families or communities where there is poverty, abuse, bullying, or trauma. These students probably surprise us with their resilience developed in response to the challenges they face. They might also display toxic stress, which can disrupt development and cause learning problems.

We create a safe, affirming and enriching learning environment for these students. This leads to better emotional regulation, a growth mindset, and more favorable learning outcomes, as psychologist Sue Roffey pointed out:

> Connected kids learn the relational values of respect, kindness, honesty, and trust. This gives them a great advantage in developing healthy and sustaining

1. Sanders, *Memoirs*, 12.

relationships in their lives, one of the most significant pillars of authentic happiness.[2]

We strengthen the resolve and build people up, especially our students, when we affirm their efforts and give voice to their goals, hopes, and dreams. We also help students and their families see the relevance of everything they are learning at school. This includes, over a period of time, a number of affirming and age-appropriate roles. Ways to accomplish this include:

- Monitor academic achievement.

- Teach knowledge skills and experiences that students can use in all aspects of their lives.

- Teach the power of personalized learning—include goal setting, planning, monitoring, and evaluating.

- Build students' self-esteem.

- Provide students with wide-ranging experiences to assist them in their future.

- Teach extracurricular activities and social skills. These include significant life skills students require for their futures, as well as basic relational, conflict resolution, and emotional regulation skills.

The plasticity and adaptability of students' brains continually changes as they undergo these different learning experiences in and out of school, which is why consistent and positive interactions between students, parents, and teachers are so important.

An affirming Christmas wartime message to the people of England, attributed to King George VI but written by Minnie Louise Haskins in 1908, inspires us to continue modeling Christian values and beliefs despite challenging times:

> I said to the man who stood at the gate of the year, 'Give me a light that I may walk safely into the unknown.' And the man said, 'Put your hand in the hand of God. That will be better than light and safer than a known way.'

2. Street and Porter, *Better Than OK*, 123.

Past students remembered their math and science teacher Siya when he died. They recalled his sense of humor, his care and compassion, his brilliant mind and the fun he brought into class: "Gentle Giant—thank you for instilling passion for numbers and science instead of fear. Primary reason why I chose the career I am in. Your legend and legacy will continue to shine for ages to come." (Sebastian) "You have shaped us to be prepared for the future we now call today." (Lily) "I cry a gentle tear as I remember how he inspired us. He made numbers magical and I send his legacy on in the teachings to my son." (Chris)

Shine a light in the darkness of others

How brightly are you shining with the love and truth of Jesus?

Effective teachers affirm life and further its potential. When we affirm others, we acknowledge their uniqueness. We become their non-judgmental and compassionate cheerleaders. Genuine affirmations used consistently change students' actions and attitudes: "You are capable of doing anything you set out to do." "You are a valuable and important member of this team." "You are amazing!"

We seek to radiate light wherever we are and give meaning to the reassuring voice of Jesus: "You are the light of the world. A town built on a hill cannot be hidden" (Matt 5:14).

We selflessly serve others and are an affirming light when we invest time and energy in their lives. Good teaching techniques inspire and intrinsically motivate, develop and encourage, and are flexible and tolerant of different opinions. We encourage students to find their voices, and guide, affirm, and empower them. As we do these things, we observe how these young people start to perform at a higher level.

We are transformative teachers as we speak to the potential that a student or colleague seems unable to see at the time (1 Sam 16:7, 1 Pet 3:8).

I worked closely alongside a colleague Dawn for a number of years. Dawn was a more effective teacher and leader than she appreciated. I realized that one of my key guiding roles was to affirm and encourage her gifts and talents. I watched her develop an incredible team of teachers around her. Every time I saw her with young students, I also observed how magnificently she facilitated teams of children who loved being in her presence. When I left the school, she wrote: "There is so much for which I am grateful. I can truly say that under your guidance I feel I have grown professionally, personally and spiritually—probably because of the example you set and the space you gave me. I shall always value the confidence you showed in me which, in turn, boosted my own self-confidence and got me "to fly." Thank you for the care and concern you have always shown me as my boss, my colleague and my friend."

Daily conversations with God

How do you experience God's affirmations? How many ways of affirming others can you think of?

God meets our individual and collective needs and makes each one of us in his divine image as a free person able to make choices. He came to earth in human form to live among his people. He affirms us through birth, death, resurrection and the ascension of Jesus. He offers us a new future. He affirms us by sending his Holy Spirit to guide and encourage us. He always walks ahead of us, remains by our side, and follows behind us. Each day, as we set time aside to consult with God, we thank him for his presence in our lives.

We affirm others just as God affirms us, because affirmation is a positive act that inspires, gives confidence, and reassures others.

Twice a week, in a school where I worked, I sent staff an email containing a Bible verse, a comment on the verse, and a thought for the day to affirm and encourage them. "It may not seem like it, but like me, I am sure lots of other people look and read these and even look forward to seeing something inspiring with a stable message of hope, belief, and encouragement in the midst of what seems like constant change at times; easily overlooked as a stabilizing influence! Sometimes the small things are the big things. I appreciate what you do and thank God for your presence at [this school]." (Tom, a colleague)

"It's been such a blessing for these to be the first emails I read in the morning. This week particularly it felt like heaven was speaking directly to my heart." (Lesley, a colleague)

Jesus always encouraged others, including his disciples, right up until his death. There are times we are asked to stand tall for our faith and go it alone, as Jesus did, with the reassurance that he will affirm our efforts (1 Thess 5:16–18, Heb 3:6, Jas 3:8–18).

"And we know that in all things God works for the good of those who love him, who have been called according to his purpose" (Rom 8:28).

Create peace in the busyness

How often do you feel overwhelmed with the pressures in your life—the demands of teaching and family, the challenges of a hostile secular environment, or the variety of pressures you experience?

How often do you skip your daily time of reading the Bible and prayer with the excuse that you have too much on or are too tired?

Most of us, if we are honest, can identify times when we have "short-changed" God.

The following activity keeps us focused on the reason we are on this planet—to become the best person God created us to be to fulfill his greater purpose.

Reflection: The three-to-five minutes Give God a Chance activity

Aim: To create a sense of peace in the busyness of your day

Time: As many times a day as you feel the need

Key outcome: To know the unconditional love, grace, peace, and affirmation of God in your life no matter the circumstances

Activity:

- Pause.
- Take a few deep breaths, rid yourself of the clutter in your life, and allow God into your space.
- Is he saying anything to you?
- Quietly pray with thanks and gratitude: "I am loved. I trust you, Lord."
- Take ownership of these statements as you reaffirm your faith.

Continue, in his presence, to recommit your life to God. Genuinely take ownership of these reassuring truths for his followers, who know that they never walk alone: "I am lovable." "I am capable."

Shine a light in a secular environment

We *are* able to make a positive difference in the lives of those with whom we interact in a secular environment. We *can* do God's work even though we might not be able to talk openly about his work (Eph 5:8, 1 John 5:14). "Preach the Gospel at all times and when necessary use words." (St Francis of Assisi)

We shine our light as people of integrity in hostile secular environments. Dr Helen Street reinforces the importance of integrity in our relationships with others:

> Honesty and trust are two of the greatest virtues of a civilized society. Along with sincerity and integrity they provide freedom, community, and safety . . . [which] probably lead to healthier, happier choices.[3]

Grace taught in a secular school where I was the principal. She knew I was a Christian. Occasionally, she wrote me a note of encouragement, which always included a Bible verse. Grace was a powerful Christian colleague and witness.

Ideas for shining our light in a secular environment

There are a variety of ways to project God's affirming light into our environments and so it is important to remain in a prayerful space throughout the day. God gently nudges us to say or do something, or maybe even seize an opportunity to share our life story, which might include our spiritual journey.

Teachers who work in secular environments face a multitude of challenges. Students are perceptive and curious. They will ask questions as they seek answers to anything that concerns or intrigues them.

Mentoring expert Marc Freedman reminds us of key roles teachers can play in the lives of their students:

> A great many young people require support that is developmental, nurturing, protective and extensive in nature—in other words, something resembling supplemental parenting. They need this caring not only to survive emotionally under adverse conditions but also to make the basic transition to adulthood.[4]

Examples of how we can shine our affirming Christian light (Phil 2:12–18) in secular environments:

1. Wear a cross. At the secular school where I was the principal and also lived, a group of female students from one of the

3. Street, *Contextual Wellbeing*, 102.
4. Freedman, *The Kindness of Strangers*, 110

hostels approached my wife and asked her if she would lead a weekly Bible study. They had seen her wearing a gold cross and had assumed she was a Christian.

2. Have a water bottle, tea or coffee mug, or lunch box with a Bible verse or Christian symbol inscribed on it.

3. Wear Christian jewelry or have a Christian keyring.

4. Use Christian stationery such as a paper weight or place a daily Christian calendar on your school desk.

5. Wear Christian clothing such as headgear or a T-shirt for extracurricular activities.

6. Place a Christian message or some other Christian insignia on your car or mode of transport, on the cover of your diary, laptop, cell phone, or school bag.

7. Promote weekly certificates of appreciation to staff nominated by colleagues, or suggest other positive ways to affirm significant contributions that reflect the school's values.

8. Carry out random acts of kindness that place the focus on others.

9. Organize surprise parties to celebrate a birthday or a special occasion.

10. Organize a fundraiser, for example an Easter egg raffle, with proceeds donated to a charity supporting disadvantaged children.

11. Play Christian music quietly in your classroom at the beginning and end of the day, where possible, and during lunch breaks.

Create your personal library of affirmations and positive memories

Do you collect affirming notes from colleagues, parents, and students? How do you motivate yourself through challenging times or times of self-doubt?

During different seasons of my life I have kept a journal to record my thoughts and ideas. This practice reminds me how God journeys with me, opens and closes doors, makes sense of confusing times, guides me to be an effective team player, blesses me in amazing ways, and *never* leaves me to face anything alone.

I have created scrapbooks capturing the positive memories of my teaching, coaching, and mentoring journeys. When I feel discouraged or question myself, the affirming words of others inspire and motivate me to continue responding to God's call on my life.

Recently I was paging through one of these scrapbooks and came across an email from Dylan, which reminded me of one of the most humbling experiences of my teaching career. Dylan was one of the many diverse personalities in my history class. The students worked hard and we had many laughs. Twenty years later Dylan received a significant business award for the work he had undertaken serving disadvantaged communities, and encouraging the growth of small businesses. His business approach continues to involve the development of cohesive teams, and promotes an entrepreneurial spirit. He wrote:

> Simply put you have been the single most influential person in my choice of course in life. Rather extreme, but to explain . . . coming from a conservative . . . family into a [school] world of commercial conformity, through your teaching and conduct you made me realize how crucial it is to question the world as it is presented to us, and from that, to decide whether the "as it is" is what we would like it to be. The final step from there would come in our action in making the change. This of course does no good unless the principle base from which this is decided is in itself whole . . . the debt I carry to you in giving me the basis on which to conduct my life is immense. So, after all that, what I really wanted to say was, thank you.

Six key strategies of an affirming teacher

1. Catch students (and colleagues) doing good things and affirm them—in the school corridors, on the sports fields, in cultural or music groups, in the classroom, or in an outreach project. Short, powerful, genuine statements are life-changing: "Congratulations! That was a great effort today." "What a good idea. Thanks for sharing it with us." "Your behavior has really improved—keep it up." "That is fantastic!" "Wow! You have figured it out—well done!" "Well done! Your persevering attitude is being rewarded." "I appreciated the way you helped your friend with her work today."

   A colleague Stephanie provided me with a moment of humility when she shared this affirming observation: "There is one specific thing that I will always remember about you, and that is the swiftness with which you praised and/or thanked me for my involvement in whichever area I had been busy. You have been a wonderful example to me of someone who is quick to thank and slow to find fault."

2. Create certificates or other mementos to affirm students who are making good progress, especially acknowledging the efforts of the weaker students. Ensure that your praise genuinely supports the intrinsic motivation of the students and they will respond positively.

3. Purchase or create motivational and fun posters with affirming and age-appropriate quotes that you can display if you have your own classroom or office. These are valuable food for the souls of bored students and reflect your values and beliefs. "I am kind." "I am helpful." "I feel good about myself and my positive friends." "I am caring." "I can learn anything; I can know anything; I can be anything." "I am chasing *my* dream!" "There *is* a solution to every problem." "I am loved." Any of these statements could lead to a discussion with a student about your faith walk.

4. Students value feedback from handwritten notes or comments at the end of projects, congratulatory or encouraging cards, fun and affirming stickers when you return work (all ages!), and recognition public or otherwise. Older students always appreciate a congratulatory letter or a reference to attach to a resume or include in a portfolio.

5. Mix up the marking pen colors, where applicable. Consider what the symbolism of red means to most students. Look to write a corrective *and* affirming comment each time you return a student's work. Address the comment to the student's first name. "Holly, you are a great student and are capable of doing anything you set your mind to." "Congratulations, Doug! I can see you have put a lot of time and effort into this project." "Stan, you are a highly capable student and when you . . ." "Charlotte, there are increasingly positive signs of the amount of time and effort you have . . ."

6. Use stories to share values and provide ways to affirm and motivate others to achieve their goals. Repetition is good for brain development, so repeat stories linked to values like humility, loyalty, community, hard work, empathy, humor, love, truthfulness, tolerance, and personal integrity.

   It takes humans 24 repetitions to get to 80% of competence. Repetition also builds mastery and synaptogenesis (develops synapses in the brain). (Andrew Fuller) [5]

MOVERS AND SHAKERS

The stories of Florence Nightingale and Billy Graham provide two interesting accounts of how God enters the lives of individuals from completely different backgrounds at the age of sixteen, and how their decision to respond to his call and shine an affirming light into the darkness of others has had a significant and positive global impact. Their lives give meaning to the belief of businessman

5. Fuller, *Re-inventing schools*, 2.

and entrepreneur Peter Legge: "when your passion and your talent intersect, you are unstoppable."

Florence Nightingale (1820–1910), The Lady with the Lamp, who made her rounds of wounded soldiers at night during the Crimean War, was an English social reformer and the founder of modern nursing. Florence grew up in a wealthy home and was home-schooled. When she was about sixteen years of age, she believed that God was calling her to devote her life in service to the suffering. This she did with immense courage, a wonderful example of an affirming servant leadership style.

> Live your life while you have it. Life is a splendid gift.
> There is nothing small in it. For the greatest things grow
> by God's law out of the smallest. But to live your life you
> must discipline it. (Florence Nightingale)

Billy Graham (1918–2018) was an American evangelist and an ordained Southern Baptist Minister. He was among the most influential leaders of the twentieth century. Billy was the son of strong Christian parents. At the age of sixteen, Billy committed his life to serve Jesus at a revival meeting held at his home and led by a travelling evangelist, Reverend Mordecai Ham. Billy's simple and direct message of sin and salvation was delivered at mass rallies. These crusades gave him international status, yet he remained a humble, obedient, godly servant leader throughout his ministry, always the affirming signpost for God's followers to meet Jesus at the foot of the cross.

> No man ever loved like Jesus. He taught the blind to see
> and the dumb to speak. He died on the cross to save us.
> He bore our sins. And now God says, 'Because he did, I
> can forgive you.' (Billy Graham)

Your talent is God's gift to you. What you do with it is your gift back to God.

—LEO BUSCAGLIA, EDUCATOR

Anyone can take children to the classroom, but only a teacher can lead them to learn. They must feel that liberty is theirs. They must feel the flush of the victory and they must feel the heart sinking of disappointment. They must feel these things . . . This was the very center of Teacher's work with me: to lessen my physical dependence on her and make it possible for me to someday continue my work without her. Teacher believed in me and I have resolved not to betray her faith. Conscious of her always, I have sought for new ways to give life to men and women whom darkness, silence, sickness, and sorrow are wearing away. It seems my teacher who touched my night flame is still about her work, using me to kindle other fires for good.

—HELEN KELLER, SPEAKING OF ANNE SULLIVAN

Children are the wet cement. Whatever falls on them makes an impression.

—HAIM GINOTT, CHILD PSYCHOLOGIST

Success is peace of mind, which is a direct result of self-satisfaction in knowing you made the effort to become the best of which you are capable.

—JOHN WOODEN, BASKETBALL COACH

Mindset change is not about picking up a few pointers here and there. It's about seeing things in a new way. When people change to a growth mindset, they change from a judge-and-be-judged framework to a learn-and-help-learn framework. Their commitment is to growth, and growth takes plenty of time, effort and mutual support.

—CAROL DWECK, PROFESSOR OF PSYCHOLOGY

CHAPTER 7

Teamwork

Do your little bit of good where you are; it's those little bits of
good put together that overwhelm the world.

—Desmond Tutu, Anglican cleric

REFLECTION

REFLECT ON YOUR DAY. Where was it difficult to find God in your
teaching today? Why was this? Were you trying to do something
in your own strength? Were you feeling overwhelmed, threatened,
or too tired to cope? Was there a colleague or someone else you
could have asked for help or shared your experience with? Allow
God to speak into your experience, to guide, heal, or reassure you.
Remember that you are never alone. Turn your prayer into a commitment to serve God as best as you can, a positive member of his
global team.

PRACTICAL STRATEGIES

What sort of team player are you? How will your students and colleagues rate you as a team player? What strengths do you bring
to the team? How can you use your unique strengths to further
benefit your team?

Imagine we are watching an orchestra at work. We see and hear the members of the orchestra creating beautiful music. We observe their individuality at times and their different skills. We admire and respect how the members appear to dance to a collaborative tune. Mutual trust and respect between the orchestra members, commitment to the needs of the group, and effective and appropriate communication are evident.

This is a great example of teamwork in action. A focused and energetic conductor skillfully brings together the talents of individuals to produce their common goal, in this case a musical score. The orchestra's teamwork helps them to complete the task professionally, collaboratively, and efficiently after a number of rehearsals.

Theologian and author Oswald Chambers used this music analogy when describing the apostle Paul's relationship to God:

> Paul was like a musician who gives no thought to audience approval, if he can only catch a look of approval from his Conductor.[1]

Teachers, like the orchestra members, are most effective when they work collaboratively with students, their families, and colleagues to offer every student the best holistic education journey possible.

In addition, teachers are like the energetic conductor as they skillfully create a safe and secure teaching environment in which students experience a sense of belonging and feel connected. And, most important, teachers choose the time and melody all can dance to each day.

Create positive partnerships

These partnerships work most effectively when we know something about our team and class members—their skills, interests, learning styles, and strengths. This takes time to develop. When we facilitate collaborative play and learning opportunities in our

1. Reimann, *My Utmost for His Highest*, March 17.

classes, for example, we quickly gather information about our students that enhances our relationships with them.

We observe students as young people with ideas, feelings, and experiences. We guide them to appreciate and understand that *how* they communicate and relate to one another is critical to the success of the team, no matter what the task might be. We help them appreciate that teamwork includes the ability to build value into the group. "We" comes ahead of "I" in our conversations.

James achieved international sporting accolades beyond school. He shared these thoughts with me a few years after he had completed his schooling: "I would like to thank you for your tremendous ability and enthusiasm that you portrayed as a coach. Without you the team would not have been the same. I would also like to thank you for helping me, as an individual, to improve my game and realize that hockey is a team game and unless you play it as a team game, you will achieve nothing and your skills will be wasted and your enjoyment for the game will decrease."

Reflect on how Jesus trained his twelve specially selected followers as a team for three years. He provides us with the perfect model of commitment, humility, empathy, tolerance of a variety of viewpoints, forgiveness, and the expression of unconditional love. He never took his eyes off his life goal and he overcame numerous obstacles.

Confront the obstacles

How prepared and equipped are you to deal with the obstacles that fall in your path and that could negatively impact your role in the team?

These obstacles take a variety of forms: personal relationship issues inside and outside the school; feeling overloaded with work; a continually disruptive student; health issues; struggling as a Christian to find your place in a secular environment; dealing with emotional pain; financial pressures; coping with death or a personal loss; or having challenging discussions with difficult parents.

In John's gospel, Jesus reminds us that life is challenging when we seek to obey his command to develop a Christian community: "Greater love has no one than this: to lay down one's life for one's friends" (John 15:13).

However, he reassures us of our vocation to go out, with love, and "bear fruit." When we draw on God's resources and obey his commands, we fulfill the call he has placed on our lives: "You did not choose me, but I chose you and appointed you so that you might go and bear fruit—that will last—and so that whatever you ask in my name the father will give you. This is my command: Love each other" (John 15:16–17).

We always find a way forward, no matter what our circumstances might be, because God is a good God who only wants the best for each one of us and his timing is perfect (2 Cor 6:3–10, Heb 12:1–13).

Ella was a quiet girl. While never in the top five, she was never far off. Her English teacher Bill enjoyed her class participation, energy, and enthusiasm. One day in ninth grade she asked Bill if she could have an Italian/German/English Dictionary from the school library. Bill spoke to a library staff member and Ella's request was granted. The following year Ella asked Bill if she could learn Italian and if he would sponsor her. Bill happened to have his hair cut by an Italian-speaking hairdresser. They conversed, made plans and found a sponsor for Ella's Italian classes. On completing her schooling, Ella was unable to find sponsorship for university education so she did Italian Intermediate. The following year she was awarded a full scholarship to university to study accounting. She also began to learn Chinese and hoped to study Korean after two years of Chinese, as she could see the advantage of learning these languages for her career plans.

Ella was sponsored by a charitable organization from a small school of thirty disadvantaged students whose parents worked at a chicken pie factory. This is a wonderful example of compassionate and caring teamwork, facilitated by a teacher who saw Ella's potential. Bill supported an ambitious young girl with dreams.

We will experience personal struggles and challenges within our teams (Mic 6:6–8). Our faith and self-discipline allow God to minister to us in our solitude. Satan's taunts are unable to gain a foothold in our lives (Heb 11:1). "It is your fault." "You are not good enough." "Why do you waste your time doing that?" "Who cares what you think?" "What do you know?" "You have always been a loser—now face up to it!"

It is normal for us to question our faith. Why did that student get so sick? Why is that child being abused? Why did my colleague die so young? Why is there so much suffering and poverty? Why is this happening to me? Where are you God?

The British evangelist David Watson wrote a book *Fear No Evil* while he was dying of cancer, a wonderful story of having faith and trust in God at all times:

> God offers no promise to shield us from the evil of this fallen world. There is no immunity guaranteed from sickness, pain, sorrow or death. What he does pledge is his never-failing presence for those who have found him in Christ. Nothing can destroy that. Always he is with us. And, in the long run, that is all we need to know.[2]

Sit at the feet of Jesus

Jesus teaches us how to overcome our fears and be witnesses of hope when we sit at his feet. We share our deepest thoughts and feelings, joys and hurts in our vulnerability at this most intimate place (Phil 4:4–6, 1 John 4:18). We appreciate Paul's message to the Philippians: "And the peace of God, which transcends all understanding, will guard your hearts and your minds in Christ Jesus" (Phil 4:7).

Jesus shares God's promises to us when he talks about the vine and the branches in John 15: "I am the true vine, and my Father is the gardener" (John 15:1).

2. Watson, *Fear no Evil,* 159.

These encouraging words highlight the importance of close and trusting partnerships in our relationships with Jesus and others.

Jesus continues, using the analogy of the vine and the role of the gardener, to reassure us that when we are connected to him, we receive his unconditional love and grace. Jesus fills us with the power of the Holy Spirit, allowing us to bear much fruit—to be his voice speaking into the lives of others, nurturing, pruning, and mentoring, a key member of his team (Gal 5:22–26).

Author and educator John Holt encouraged teachers to think of themselves as gardeners: "A gardener does not grow flowers; he tries to give them what he thinks will help them grow, and they grow by themselves. A child's mind, like a flower, is a living thing. We can't make it grow by sticking things into it any more than we can make a flower grow by gluing on leaves and petals. All we can do is surround the growing mind with what it needs for growing and have faith that it will take what it needs and grow."

Life in Christ

A key message of this book is that life in Christ is best lived and identified in daily union with him (2 Tim 8:16). We are members of his team, sharing equal status with all the other team members. Ranks, titles, and positions of authority mean nothing when it comes to our relationship with Jesus (Gal 2:6).

We persevere in prayer and remain one with him at all times, especially when we are tested (Phil 2:4). These times test our commitment, as transformative teachers, to follow Jesus no matter the cost. This is especially true when we move out of our comfort zones, as Lucy often did during her wonderful teaching career.

Lucy was a teacher with a deep Christian faith. She reminisced on her years as a teacher in secular schools: "The kind of things that made my teaching worthwhile were small. The kids who told me I was their favorite teacher or the ones who came and shared stuff from home. I often worked with less privileged kids. I got a lot of rewards from the kids I introduced to squash, especially those [from high-risk environments], and took them to tournaments. One who stands out was a promising young rugby player who lost an arm in a motorbike accident at sixteen. I introduced him to squash and it turned his life around."

Build community

How effectively do you build community?

God's Spirit manifests itself through our fruit as we selflessly reach out to a student or a colleague in need. We offer a kind word or action, celebrate someone else's success, or help resolve a conflict scenario. We show self-control when a recalcitrant student, or aggressive parent, or a cynical colleague tests us. We display the patience of Job when we face any challenging situation. We work tirelessly behind the scenes in support of a worthy cause.

These are expressions of God's love in action. "Love is a fruit in season at all times and within the reach of every hand." (Mother Teresa)

Effective schools showcase an atmosphere of authentic care for one another. There is a sense of selfless teamwork. Teaching and non-teaching colleagues are dedicated to the school's vision and mission, and work collaboratively to create an atmosphere of happiness, safety, and excitement that a visitor senses when they set foot on the campus. I experienced this in one school when a visitor commented: "There is something special here. I can feel it."

We build community when we use our strengths and God-given talents to grow others, sometimes at great personal cost. We are the bridge to Jesus through our attitudes and actions, often without realizing that this is occurring (1 Pet 4:10–11).

I invited a colleague Alex, who had discovered a student abusing alcohol at a school event, to join the disciplinary team process to help her personal development. She later wrote: "Thank you for letting me be there through the whole process of involving me in all the lengthy discussions. I learned a lot about being fair, about procedure and about taking an objective, unbiased stand

(and more). Thank you for your patience and wisdom, and the chance you gave me to learn more about dealing with teenagers."

Alex shared her experience with colleagues and possibly part of that experience with other students. The community was strengthened, as was Alex's faith journey.

Walk in the footsteps of Jesus

What team footprint will you leave behind? What signs of servant leadership do others witness?

Students and colleagues observe our every move. We express our faith in obedience to his will (Rom 12:1–12), in the way we think, and what we do and say. We understand that unity in Christ transcends ethnic, social, and gender distinctions (Gal 3:28).

Effective Christian teachers have godly characters. They are seed sowers with a clear vision of what is attained with a nurturing approach. They create the best possible conditions for growth, build trust, and ignite the fire in others to achieve their dreams. These teachers continually work on self-development; respect the aims, concerns, and circumstances of all team members; constantly and honestly assess the progress in a change process (a time of uncertainty when venturing into the unknown); give responsibilities to others, and walk in the footsteps of Jesus (Mark 4:1–20).

I spent a few years working with Abby, a creative and talented teacher with a great sense of humor, who at times lacked confidence as a leader. I supported and encouraged Abby to develop a positive team approach in the areas of her responsibility. She wrote: "I know we'll be a bit shaky without you as our mainstay as well as anchor, but you helped us all grow so much as individuals, in our relationships, and in our roles in management, that I know we'll rise to the challenge remembering all we have learnt. I will always remember you as a leader who helped me grow by believing in me and allowing me to make mistakes and then applying the Band-Aids. Thank you for all you've done for me and my personal growth."

Seven key strategies to co-create a strong and united community

Reflect on these ideas, which can be adapted for different age groups, to focus on the gifts and strengths of those around you as you co-create a strong and united community (1 Pet 4:10–11):

1. Train students to defer gratification, have the courage to persevere, replace a sense of entitlement with a sense of selfless service to others, and develop emotional intelligence. Guide them to use technology responsibly, to think outside the box and problem solve in teams.

2. Promote teamwork through your teaching and sharing. Students enjoy stories, anecdotes, group work, DVDs, social media clips, photos, and other visual aids, as well as humor. Vary your student-centered teaching methods to cater for team and group work which most students enjoy. Encourage cooperative learning by having students working in groups on a project and being assessed as a group. Remain mindful that the *ideal* for positive brain health is to combine both physical and mental stimulation along with social interactions, as the ability of the brain to rewire and remap itself via neuroplasticity is profound.

3. As a facilitator, encourage students to connect with school, peer groups, and the local community—different teams. As examples, view each class as a team; facilitate an extracurricular activity and share team-building strategies with the students, or facilitate an outreach activity to another school or group in the community. Learn a language of students from different cultures—words to greet, farewell, or ask non-threatening questions. Encourage students to teach you their language. They love teaching the teacher!

4. Teach students the importance of taking time out to reflect on their lives. Model non-judgmental, respectful, and empathetic listening.

5. Explore ways to involve parents in their children's education through parent evenings, cultural activities, and sport. Phone, email, or text a parent to share a compliment about their child. When you do this, you not only build community, but also build small teams of support and encouragement around every student.

6. Follow school policies and procedures. Involve other agencies in a student's life, preferably with his or her permission, when the situation of a student warrants this. A web of support (a team) is created around a vulnerable student with the help of colleagues. The community is strengthened.

7. Give students a non-threatening survey to complete when you meet a class or group of students for the first time. Ask for information like their favorite food, subject, sports, hobbies, or interests; favorite music, movies, social media platforms, apps, programs; someone they look up to and admire and why (both within and outside the family). Have them share as many answers as possible. You create a team approach and build a respectful and collaborative community.

Concluding thoughts

Our eternal mission involves obeying God's call on our lives. We stay close to him and strive each day to share the good news of the birth, life, death, resurrection, and ascension of Jesus. We share his love and the power of the Holy Spirit with others.

"And now these three remain: faith, hope and love. But the greatest of these is love" (1 Cor 13:13). My friend Brian Bird commented: "In listing those three, Paul is not only highlighting the fact that the three are of utmost importance for our spiritual journey, but he is also highlighting the intimate connection between the three. They belong together—faith, the key that opens the door into the presence and blessings of God; hope, the inspiration that encourages us to keep running the race set before us and love, the gift that transforms everything and, when expressed in our life, gives the world a sense of who Jesus is."

These chapters remind us to prioritize being kind to ourselves as we co-create a global Christian community (John 14:6, Heb 13:5).

Perhaps, like Luke, we may one day share: "I consider my life worth nothing to me; my only aim is to finish the race and complete the task the Lord Jesus has given me—the task of testifying to the good news of God's grace" (Acts 20:24). Dr Michael Cassidy suggests that our challenge is to "finish better than we started." (see Appendix 3)

At all times, reflect on the significant responsibilities you have as you invest your time and energy in the lives of the students, their families, and your colleagues, and remember another truth: Hey teacher! You *are* amazing!

MOVERS AND SHAKERS

The Christian walk is thought-provoking and interesting. It often requires us to overcome challenging obstacles. The following two stories highlight this and give meaning to the comment, "Every job is a self-portrait of the person who did it. So autograph your work with excellence."

William Wilberforce (1759–1833) is remembered as an English politician who led a team of like-minded people in a movement to abolish the slave trade and slavery throughout the British Empire. William's family were merchants. He grew up in a privileged home, went to Cambridge University, and became a Member of Parliament at the age of twenty-one. In 1784, while on a trip to Europe, he spent time with one of his former teachers who gave him a book by William Law, *A Serious Call to a Devout and Holy Life*. William's journey to commit his life to Christ was underway! When he became a Christian in 1785, this book strongly influenced his lifestyle choices. He became actively involved in social reform, most especially the abolition of slavery and the improvement of factory conditions in Britain. John Newton, a former slave ship captain and the author of *Amazing Grace*, and John Wesley, one of the founders of Methodism, significantly impacted William's Christian journey.

> I am disturbed when I see the majority of so-called Christians having such little understanding of the real nature of the faith they profess. Faith is the subject of such importance that we should not ignore it because of the distractions or the hectic pace of our lives. (William Wilberforce)

Amy Carmichael (1867–1951) was a Christian missionary in India who established the Dohnavur Fellowship, which housed troubled or threatened girls, young women, and even babies. Amy, one of seven children, was the daughter of devout Christian parents and loved the Lord from an early age. When her father died, she had to drop out of school. Amy's mission to India lasted fifty-five years. The last twenty years of her team mission were directed from her bedroom after a bad fall. Amy was also a prolific author.

> If I can write an unkind letter, speak an unkind word, think an unkind thought without grief and shame, then I know nothing of Calvary love. You can give without loving, but you cannot love without giving. (Amy Carmichael)

Some advice on listening for someone who cares from someone who needs care

You are *not listening* to me when . . .

You do not care about me.

You say you understand before you know me well enough.

You have an answer for my problem before I've finished telling you what the problem is.

You cut me off before I've finished speaking.

You finish my sentence for me.

You find me boring and don't tell me.

You feel critical of my vocabulary, grammar or accent.

You are dying to tell me something.

You tell me about your experience, making mine seem unimportant.

You are communicating to someone else in the room.

You refuse my thanks by saying you really haven't done anything.

You *are listening* to me when . . .

You come quietly into my private world and let me be me.

You really try to understand me even if I'm not making much sense.

You grasp my point of view even when it's against your own sincere convictions.

You realize the hour I took from you has left you a bit tired and drained.

You allow me the dignity of making my own decisions even though you think they may be wrong.

You do not take my problem away from me but allow me to deal with it in my own way.

You hold back your desire to give me good advice.

You do not offer me religious solace when you sense I am not ready for it.

You give me enough room to discover for myself what is really going on.

You accept my gift of gratitude by telling me how good it makes you feel to know you have been helpful.

—AUTHOR UNKNOWN

A broad outline of a student's journey of self-discovery and self-empowerment

How are you optimistically preparing your students for the real world beyond school—their journey of self-discovery and self-empowerment?

Much will depend on the age group or groups we teach. The younger students are on a journey of discovery. They are discovering more about themselves, their interests and talents, how to make friends and behave appropriately in a school or team environment, and how to respond to the issues they face every day. Primary or junior school students, for example, benefit from being allowed to decorate their classroom with their teacher and peers, rather than have the teacher create and beautify their learning area.

The responsibility we carry is significant. Research suggests that the first six years of a child's life are significant for the brain to develop fully. These students develop a sense of self. Their life experiences shape their emotional wellbeing. This is why our daily, individualized communication within a caring and nurturing environment is so important.

Peer relationships take on greater significance in the lives of students aged nine or ten. Increased incidents of bullying occur as they seek to establish their positions in groups and relationships. Aware of these changes, we establish peer relationship programs to include age appropriate discussions about bullying, emotional intelligence, and resilience. A well-structured vertical tutoring system in the middle and senior years of schooling, in which every student is supported by a tutor and a co-tutor, will prepare students for life beyond school and enhance their relationship-building skills.

Students approaching adolescence enjoy a particularly creative time in their lives as they explore different ideas and concepts. They grapple with physical and emotional changes as they look for meaning and purpose.

Students in their final years of school are preparing for the world of work, which might involve further studying. Their brains continue to develop until the mid-twenties. They start to determine the values that will powerfully impact their life choices. These values will be important as they embark on a season of independence.

Students need to develop competencies, self-confidence, and the ability to connect with others. They can then move confidently into the real world of work. Empowerment involves guiding and equipping them to feel stronger and more confident with their life choices. They learn how to respectfully stand up for their rights, as they develop meaningful relationships with God, family, and peers.

APPENDIX 3

Global Prayer for Peace[1]

IN 2016 I VISITED the Terezin Concentration Camp outside Prague. 15,000 children under the age of fifteen passed through this camp between 1942 and 1944. Fewer than one hundred children survived. I was deeply moved looking at the original drawings and poems many of these children had produced. I wrote this prayer which I pray every week.

Father God,
Embrace all nations with a vision of global peace;
Transform the hearts and minds of all people that they might capture this vision of peaceful co-existence and collaborative living
And let it begin with me.
Encourage me not to rest until I know that our global community is free and as equal as is humanly possible;
Help me to speak out with courage and boldness against discrimination and injustice;
Guide our global leaders to rid their countries of any unjust and oppressive laws, guaranteeing their people freedom of thought, religion, speech and movement;
Protect us from the evils of tyranny and the abuse of fundamental Human Rights and give me the strength to speak out against such atrocities;

1. (The Global Prayer for Peace is framed by the Declaration of Human Rights) (Robin Cox)

Raise up global leaders committed to ending war, global poverty and injustice;

Create a global village in which all peoples have the right to affordable housing, medicine, education, child-care and have sufficient money to live on;

Use me to reach out to those less privileged without expecting anything in return;

Help me to understand my duty to my fellow men, women and children and to play my small part in ensuring their freedom and rights are protected;

Gently nudge me each and every day to remember that the change begins with me;

Let me never cease striving to play my small part in establishing a global community built on freedom, justice and peace.

In the precious name of Jesus, I pray.

Amen

Acknowledgments

THIS BOOK IS THE culmination of approximately forty-five years as an educator. I have gathered quotes, notes from conferences, gold nuggets of wisdom and helpful tips from a variety of books, magazines, blogs, DVDs, websites and general conversations with people.

The content, therefore, is a tribute to the many people from a variety of backgrounds and professions who have shared their life experiences and wisdom either with me personally or with the global community.

I must make special mention of the inspirational impact Dr Michael Cassidy has had on my faith walk and on my career as a teacher. Michael founded the work of African Enterprise in South Africa with the aim of spreading the Christian message throughout the African continent. Michael inspired and motivated me to set up youth symposia to prepare young people for a post-apartheid South Africa (mentioned in the introduction) in the 1980s. He kindly wrote the foreword to my first book for young people and has been a wonderful model of humble and selfless servant leadership, ably supported by his equally talented wife Carol. Michael's autobiography, *Footprints in the African Sand: My life & times*, is a fascinating description of how God chooses yet another mover and shaker to fulfil his greater purpose.

The reflection activities at the beginning of each chapter are adapted from *The Examen*, a prayerfully reflective practice developed by St Ignatius of Loyola (1491–1556) to help us see God's hand at work in our daily life, and to learn and grow as we allow God to transform our lives. They follow an important principle of an effective teacher: the experience alone does not teach us much. However, when we reflect on the experience, we deepen our learning. Indeed, we become more Christlike.

An extensive list of resources is available on my website, www.yess.co.nz, to give readers some references for the content in this book, in addition to the sources listed in the bibliography.

If I have inadvertently failed to acknowledge a source, I would be most grateful if the reader would inform me so that I can rectify the omission.

Special thanks to the many people who read my introduction and offered feedback. There are too many names to list. You know who you are. Thank you for encouraging me to write this book, which I hope has also answered many of the questions you asked me to think about while writing.

Outside of my family, who are my greatest critics and encouragers, sincere thanks to Rudi Pakendorf and the Reverend Brian Bird.

Rudi has been my "go to" person from the time I felt called to write this book. He caught the vision and has been a mentor and prayer warrior throughout the writing and publishing journey. He has allowed me to share some wonderful thoughts and ideas that have been woven into the chapters. Our friendship, which I cherish, spans almost forty years, from the day we met as teaching colleagues.

Brian became a friend and confidant when I was a school principal in Cape Town more than twenty years ago. He challenged my thinking, moved me out of my comfort zone and helped me lead a school with a strong outreach program to disadvantaged communities. I have valued Brian's prayers and encouragement as I have been writing this book.

Both Rudi and Brian shared a similar message, which had to be from God, at a critical time of the writing of this book when I was seeking some direction. Thanks for your obedience in honestly sharing those messages.

Thanks, too, to Paul Browning, who gave me the opportunity to have my dream job at St Paul's school prior to my retirement.

Paul is a strategic thinker and visionary, a deeply committed Christian, unafraid to challenge educators to move out of their comfort zones and offer a holistic and relevant education to their students. I recommend his new book, *Principled, 10 leadership practices for building trust.*

Finally, sincere thanks to Matthew Wimer and the editors at Resource Publications of Wipf and Stock for all their support, help and guidance and, most especially, to my editor Maryanne Wardlaw for her significant contributions and expertise.

Bibliography

Brokensha, Brian. Email correspondence with Robin Cox. January 1999. Used with permission.

Cassidy, Michael. *Chasing the Wind: Man's search for life's answers.* Shuter and Shooter. 1985.

Freedman, Marc. *The Kindness of Strangers: Adult Mentors, Urban Youth, and the New Voluntarism.* Cambridge University Press. 1999.

Fuller, Andrew. *Re-inventing schools from the brain up: A discussion paper.* 2012. http://andrewfuller.com.au

Reimann, James G., ed. *My Utmost for His Highest: The Golden Book of Oswald Chambers.* Discovery House. 1992.

Sanders, Marion. *Memoirs of a Follower: Developing the art of listening to God at work.* Castle. 2018.

Street, Helen. *Contextual Wellbeing: Creating Positive Schools from the Inside Out.* Wise Solution. 2018.

Street, Helen and Porter, Neil, eds. *Better Than OK: Helping young people to flourish at school and beyond.* Freemantle. 2014.

Watson, David. *Fear No Evil.* Hodder & Stoughton, London. 1984.

Yerkes, Mary. *A Christ-Centred Model for Balanced Living.* October 24, 2014. http://christianlifecoaching.com/christ-centred-model-balanced-living.

www.ingramcontent.com/pod-product-compliance
Lightning Source LLC
Chambersburg PA
CBHW060359090426
42734CB00011B/2193